HEAVEN BOUND

HEAVEN BOUND

ONE WOMAN'S JOURNEY
from the Drug House *to*
the King's House

SHAWNTA' PULLIAM

NASHVILLE

NEW YORK   MELBOURNE

HELL BENT HEAVEN BOUND
ONE WOMAN'S JOURNEY *from the* Drug House *to the* King's House

© 2017 SHAWNTA' PULLIAM

Published in New York, New York, by Morgan James Publishing. Morgan James and The Entrepreneurial Publisher are trademarks of Morgan James, LLC.
www.MorganJamesPublishing.com

Shelfie

A **free** eBook edition is available
with the purchase of this print book.

CLEARLY PRINT YOUR NAME ABOVE IN UPPER CASE

Instructions to claim your free eBook edition:
1. Download the Shelfie app for Android or iOS
2. Write your name in **UPPER CASE** above
3. Use the Shelfie app to submit a photo
4. Download your eBook to any device

ISBN 978-1-68350-107-7 paperback
ISBN 978-1-68350-109-1 eBook
ISBN 978-1-68350-108-4 hardcover
Library of Congress Control Number:
2016908985

Cover Design by:
Rachel Lopez
www.r2cdesign.com

Interior Design by:
Bonnie Bushman
The Whole Caboodle Graphic Design

In an effort to support local communities, raise awareness and funds, Morgan James Publishing donates a percentage of all book sales for the life of each book to Habitat for Humanity Peninsula and Greater Williamsburg.

Get involved today! Visit
www.MorganJamesBuilds.com

Contents

Foreword

It has been said that everything happens for a reason. This phrase is so common that many consider it a cliché. All of us have asked the age-old questions of "Why am I here?" or "Why was I created?" Some of us may have gone nearly a lifetime with these questions left buried and unanswered within us. Perhaps if we realized that we weren't created for ourselves, then words like *impossible* and *fail* wouldn't exist in our vocabulary. Take a moment to reflect on your life and consider "What if?"

What if we were forced to look at our lives—the good, the bad, the ugly—and determine that the outcome of every experience we've ever encountered wasn't merely survival, but something far more valuable? What if wrapped beneath our deepest struggles are the makings of our biggest triumphs? What if our hardships produced a greatness within us that would have gone undiscovered had we not suffered and paid a price that cost us deeply?

Shawntá Pulliam came to a realization one day that she could no longer live life operating in "business as usual" mode. She had an epiphany and concluded that she was built for more—something far greater, something bigger and better than anything she could envision for her life. Deep inside she knew she was groomed in greatness, fashioned and designed for God's purpose!

In *Hell Bent, Heaven Bound* author Shawntá Pulliam offers a vivid account of her experience from childhood to the present, a journey that led her on a path of self-reflection and determination to find God's purpose for her life. She uncovers the ways in which God allows situations to refine us and produce His abundant purpose in our lives. If you are struggling with your existence and wondering what is in store for you, look no further! This book will serve as a demonstration and testimony of a life activated by God's purpose and plan.

Shawntá urges you to live intentionally and illustrates how experiences build and shape who we are *to be* rather than who we are *at the moment*. This book will challenge you to look ahead, beyond the fog of "here and now." It will push you to uncover roadblocks within your being and honestly ask the question "What's stopping me from accomplishing my dreams?" Get ready to function-on-purpose and discover the life of success that you were born to live!

—Les Brown
Motivational Speaker/Trainer/Author

Chapter 1

Created for God's Purpose

"STAT!" the doctors yelled as they rushed my mother through winding hallways toward the emergency room. She needed an emergency C-section or they would lose us both. The problem was, I was trapped in the womb. My mother could not dilate. She prayed and pushed, pushed and prayed again, but nothing.

"O God, please let my little girl live," Mom whispered in between tears. "Please, God."

"Room three!" The attending physician pointed to the first available bed.

My mother's feet were still in those cold steel stirrups. Alarms from the monitors sang a chorus as my mother's vital signs moved dangerously too low for either of us to survive. Why was this happening? It would be many years before I found the answer. The enemy knew what God

1

had placed inside of me. The only way for him to cut off my future was to prevent me from getting here in the first place. He knew I would be a weapon to tear down his kingdom. He knew I would come into the world with the unusual power given to me from the hand of an almighty God.

So on that day Satan drew a line in the sand. Hell made plans for my demise—but heaven made plans for my success. Heaven's plans were for my mother and me to live and not die. In an instant, angels surrounded us, God's angels of healing mercy. I was born, and through my birth hell was defeated.

I knew from that day forward that no matter how trapped, how stuck, how suffocated, or how bad life might appear, the enemy could do us no harm. For you, it may seem as if there is no way out of your situation, but God always provides a way of escape. He did it for me, and He will do it for you.

No matter how lost, confused, rejected, abused, and scared your life has been, or may seem now, you—yes YOU—were born for God's purpose. Your relationship with God may not be exactly where you would like it to be, or on a level that you feel most comfortable with, but God uses those emotions of emptiness and feelings of scarcity to show the power of His love and reveal His purpose in your life. He fills our void with His presence.

In Jeremiah 1:5, we hear these words: "Before I formed you in the womb I knew you, before you were born I set you apart." Jeremiah questioned his purpose in fear and doubt. Did that change his calling? No. God had a plan for him, and God wanted Jeremiah to know Him and trust in Him. God uses us when we feel useless. Yes, He knew you would be raised without a father, or have a mother you could not confide in. God knew your parents would not be there for you emotionally when you needed them most. He knew people would hurt, use, abuse, and mistreat you. Through all of your struggles and shortcomings, through the lack and depravity, you are still here. That is your miracle—you are still here.

As we go through daily struggles, we tend to forget the purpose God has placed on our lives. We forget His love and mercy. He can seem to be nowhere, leaving us to question His very existence and the safety and security that can be found in His arms.

As a child, I never quite understood God. I wondered, *Who is this Man my grandmother clings to at night as she bends her knees, folds her hands, and closes her eyes?* She called to Him when my cousin was in the streets on drugs again. I would kneel beside Grandma and repeat what she taught me, in hopes to bring my cousin home safely that night, to ease the pain of my nightmares of him being found dead in the street.

At the age of five, I would recite, "Now I lay me down to sleep, I pray the Lord my soul to keep, if I should die before I wake, I pray the Lord my soul to take," and I always added my closing: "and God bless everybody, amen." Although I was young, I could feel His presence after I finished my prayer; a still peace would come over my tiny little body, confirming that everything would be all right. It was as if I had a greater sensitivity to His presence. I'd like to think it was an overflow from the day I was born and the struggles God brought me through in that hospital room.

I was a quiet child, very observant and analytical, which made me seem kind of weird, but that was the wiring I needed to have for God to use me later in life. Perhaps you had a peculiar personality as a child. As you discover God's purpose for your life, He will reveal why He made you that way, and it will all make sense as you uncover your God-given gifts and calling.

As for me, my quietness was a reflection of wisdom, my observation was a reflection of discernment, and my analyzing was a reflection of problem solving. God uses the things we do not like most about ourselves—or those things we are confused about—and breathes purpose into them, but we have to submit to His way of thinking through prayer, meditation, reading, and believing His Word.

Did you know you being here on earth resulted from a "great race"? When you were being conceived, God chose you during the process out of millions of other possibilities. You probably remember from science class that only the fastest and strongest sperm gets to unite with the egg to form a human being and be a part of this earth, and that unique combination of DNA was you! No matter what may have happened to you in your life, or how you got here, you were not a mistake. You are a part of God's plan, and He wants to use you to do great and miraculous things on this earth. In spite of all the negative things you may see within yourself, God sees Himself in you, but you have to see yourself in God and anchor yourself in His love.

Many people do not believe they are special, created for a purpose. You may even feel this way because perhaps you were adopted, or your mother was a victim of rape. I have friends whose parents told them they were a mistake. God does not make mistakes. Your parents may have had other plans in your absence, or maybe they were unable to raise you or raise you properly, the way your heart yearned. Whatever the situation, none of that matters because God wanted you here. His love birthed you, regardless of anything to the contrary.

When I look back over my life, if I did not know God as I do now, I would question whether He loved me or even existed.

I came from a very loving extended family that lived in a huge house. The household consisted of me, my mom, my grandma, my cousin, and my uncle. My parents were married, and my mother always shared with me how my father was a very sweet, loving man. She told me how he would polish her toenails when her stomach became too big while she was pregnant. He would give her baths and cater to her every need. They had a very strong love—best friends, some would say. She shared how they would ride on double banana-seat bikes in the sun, dressed in matching T-shirts and sunglasses. But when people took notice of how happy and strong their family was, many became envious and wanted to split them up.

Because my dad was happy and loved his wife and was not afraid to let others know, the female home wreckers came to destroy my family, and as Eve convinced Adam to disobey God, these women tempted my father, and he fell into lust. He became abusive to my mother in defense of his infidelity. Eventually my mother had enough and divorced my father when I was only five years old.

After their divorce, I only saw small flashes of my father. Once in a while he would pop up with a gift—when he was not incarcerated.

There I was at five, missing a very important link in my life, the love of a father, the genuine love of a man. Throughout my life, this haunted me mentally and emotionally. It was evident as I unwittingly chose men who reflected my father's dark side, but thankfully God revealed to me His light and love. He showed me that although I had grown up without knowing the love of a father or love from a man I had not been physically intimate with, I could lean on Him to be the Love I needed to feel safe, secure, and wanted. God used this missing part of my life to draw me closer to Him and to show me that the ultimate Father and source is Him.

Philippians 4:19 says: "My God shall supply all your needs according to His riches in glory in Christ Jesus." Notice He says "all," meaning you shall lack for nothing; everything that has been missing in your life God will supply for you, if you believe and allow Him to heal every empty void in your life.

Yes, you may still yearn for the love of an absent father, mother, husband, or wife, but God will give you peace and joy while they are absent and comfort you through the Holy Spirit; He will even bring other people and angels to fill that void. There are no limits to what God can do. Whatever is missing in your life, God is waiting to replace it. All you have to do is ask.

Take a few minutes and ask God to fill the empty part of you that you may have had while growing up or any emptiness you may feel today. He is waiting to give you that love you have been craving. He created you specifically to have a loving relationship with Him. Matthew 22:37-38 says that our greatest command by God is to "Love the Lord your God with all your heart and with all your soul and with all your mind. This is the first and greatest commandment."

Let Him in. He has your purpose in His hands and is waiting for you to fall into His arms and receive what He purposed for you before He created the heavens and the earth. He was thinking of you way back then and couldn't wait to give you His Love.

Flashes of Purpose

Flashes of purpose are those little scenarios you had while growing up that you may have ignored. As a child, perhaps you saw those close to you praying or attending church services. Those flashes of purpose were God showing you the way to everlasting life. Maybe it was the Bible that sat on your living room table, or the Gospel channels on the television, or a neighbor up the street, or the mom of a friend who had an unapologetic love for God.

The Bible says, "Raise up a child in the direction he will go, and when he is old, he will not depart from it." Notice how it says "when he is old" (this refers to both genders). I took some time to ponder and pray on that, and what God revealed to me was that at some point when the child is young they may very well depart from it, but once they come back to who they are—and the foundation they were rooted and grounded in—when they are older they will not depart from it. They will remember and cling to it.

There was a point in my life, during my college years, when I departed from God. College introduces you to theory and philosophy, contradicting everything you have learned about Jesus. If you are not spiritually mature, you can be easily swayed from the very source of your existence.

However, my foundation ran deep as these flashes of purpose began when I was eight years old. I would be outside, all dressed up with my Jerry curls bouncing on the top of my head, practicing my dance moves with my friends for the annual street dance. The street dance was something we all looked forward to. It was an opportunity to show our talents through song and dance. I was the best mover on my block when it came to dancing, and I made sure I practiced every day. I picked out the outfits that our group would wear, which of course always had to match.

As we were outside shaking our butts to the boom box sitting on the top step of the sun porch, Sister Lou would come by. Sister Lou was an old black lady around seventy-five, but in excellent shape. She wore a blue-and-white nun's habit and a head wrap and hood around her head that reminded me of pictures of Harriet Tubman. She walked with a long wooden cane in the "hood" where we lived and preached the gospel to adults and even children. She would knock from door to door and ask to come in and have prayer and "church"; some people would let her in while others would not, but it did not matter to her. She just shook the dust off her feet and kept on doing what God had told her to do.

If there were an example of the fear of Jesus on earth, Sister Lou would be that example. People would see her coming and hide beer cans, drop cigarettes, immediately stop cussing, and act in their best behavior; some people would cry out and ask for prayer. She prophesied over people's houses and preached on corners and in the middle of the street.

I know now that Sister Lou was indeed a prophet. She and my grandmother were good friends, so while I was shaking my butt and teaching my new dance moves I had recorded off of BET onto the VCR, I knew it would not last long as I saw her walking towards our house. While my friends and I were getting warmed up and learning the latest moves, I would be immediately interrupted and told to come in the house because Sister Lou was there for prayer. My friends just stood there looking at me weirdly, rolling their eyes and heads full of beads, before running away in fear.

I was called out from among them at eight years old. Do you see the flash of purpose? God was setting me apart even then. Now the average eight-year-old would have thrown a tantrum, but even then I could feel inside of me a sense of need—that somehow being a part of the prayer service was a part of me, although I did not quite understand why.

As I walked in the house, my mom, my grandmother, and Sister Lou would be sitting there on the couch. Sister Lou always got the big tall chair. Then they would send me to the kitchen to get Sister Lou some cheese and crackers because that was her favorite. After I served her snack I would sit down.

We usually began with a song—"Jesus is on the mainline, tell Him what you want"—then a scripture, John 3:3, when Jesus told Nicodemus, a ruler of the Jews, "Very truly I tell you, none can see the kingdom of God unless he is born again." And we would pray for everyone in the family and our city.

I remember her words because it was the same scripture and prayer each time, but the vibration and power were just as powerful, if not more so. After the house service, Sister Lou would lay her hands on my little head and pray for me. After she removed her hands, I would skip back outside to my friends, who came out from behind the backyard where they were hiding and waiting for me, snickering and eager to start dancing again.

These experiences as a child were wiring me spiritually, preparing me for what was ahead. I believe my grandmother and mother knew what they were planting inside of me, but even if they did not, it didn't matter because God had the plan to flash His light that would lead me on the right path toward my purpose. The Bible says, "Be still and know that I am God," so be still, watch, listen, and pay attention to God's direction in your life. He is waiting for you to choose the right path. Rise to your assignment and know you are created for a purpose.

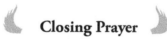

Closing Prayer

Lord, help me to be continually aware of Your presence and unfailing love for me. Whatever I lack in my life, I ask that You fill every void as I lean on and trust in You. Holy Spirit, the Spirit of all wisdom, help me to see, understand, and move on behalf of God's purpose for my life. God does not make mistakes, so I will never be a mistake. I am exactly who God wants me to be. All that I have been through and all that I am will work together for my good and God's perfect plan for my life. I will no longer look at my faults as hindrances, but as steps to where God is calling me to be. I am created for a purpose; my pain will become my power. I believe, I welcome, and I receive the manifestation of God's purpose and destiny for my life. In Jesus's name, amen.

Chapter 2

Veering Away from God

I t is often said that the reason more people are not Christian is because of Christians. Being exposed to "religious" people who have no real relationship with God is one of the biggest reasons people do not believe in God in the first place. This is the ultimate irony.

We, as fellow Christians, have to remember a very important element of spiritual life. The devil spent many eons with God before he got kicked out of heaven. He was not just praying to God; he was sitting close to God, talking to God, fellowshipping with God. What does this mean? This means the devil has unusual insight into how to create an environment that looks, feels, and sounds just like God.

This is why praying for the spirit of discernment is so critical, because the devil understands how to manipulate our senses strategically. He also plays upon the sins and flaws we have while never reminding us that Jesus has taken away the sting, through the shedding of His blood.

All types of people are in the body of Christ, which means all types of crazy people believe in God, all types of troublemakers, backbiters, gossipers, womanizers, prostitutes, manipulators, liars—feel free to add to the list any other type you have encountered throughout life.

What we fail to recognize is that the *main* reason people are in church is to better themselves, to gain a better relationship with God, and to become more like Him. Some take longer than others to grow into a level of spiritual maturity where they can be effective in the body of Christ, in their community, and to the unbeliever who is watching them to see if this "God thing" is real. While it is important to be a great example, it is far more important to communicate that God is the only true example.

Let me ask you a question: Do you turn away from your mother or father because you can't get along with your alcoholic brother?

Do you stop loving your grandmother because your uncle is a troublemaker? Of course not! So why veer away from God's love because of the mishaps of His spiritual family? Maybe they have hurt you and mistreated you, taken you for granted and lied to you, but forgiveness can be given if you trust God and want peace within yourself. We will talk more about the power of forgiveness in chapter 4.

The Bible instructs Christians to speak gently when bringing others to Christ. We as Christians must be gentle and full of love, not aggressive, critical, and forceful. That only runs people away. However, once we look past an offense and realize it is their lack of a relationship with God or a lack of spiritual growth on their part, we begin to understand just how personal a relationship with God is.

There have been so many occasions where I could have gotten offended and even disgusted, left my church, and veered away from God. I can recall a time when I was visiting churches, praying, and searching for a church home. I was emotionally drained and trying to find my way back into the body of Christ, so I joined a small storefront church. I liked the preaching, the choir, and Wednesday night's Tarry. If you are not familiar with Tarry nights, it is something you need to experience at least once in your life. Popular in apostolic churches, it includes a room full of saints who praise God for hours upon hours, kneeled on the floor before chairs. Kids as young as five and adults as old as ninety attend Tarry.

At a Tarry night, there is no music, no preaching, no singing or testimonies, just everyone in one accord with arms raised chanting "Hallelujah, Hallelujah, Hallelujah" over and over again until the spirit of tongues falls upon them and they are filled with God's Holy Spirit. You are invited into Tarry after you have been baptized. The book of Acts speaks of this.

However, at this point in my life the Holy Spirit had not fallen upon me yet, so the pastor and the women of the congregation attacked me for wearing makeup and lipstick. They told me I would not receive the Holy Spirit and any spiritual gifts because of my outward appearance.

Baffled by their confrontation, I questioned how God could hold back His love from me because I had color on my lips. How could He reject me from receiving His gift? Is God as trivial as the people representing Him? He is not. The Lord said to Samuel in 1 Samuel 16:7, "Do not consider his appearance or his height, for I have rejected him...."

This scripture makes it abundantly clear the Lord does not look at the outward appearance to qualify or disqualify a person. The Lord looks at the heart. You must keep this word in your mind and heart when people reject and judge you because of your outer appearance, or your upbringing, or where you live, how you dress, how you wear your hair, the car you drive, your makeup, and so forth. Although these things should respectfully represent God, they are not requirements for God to have a relationship with you.

Allow the Holy Spirit to Work

Scripture teaches us that the Holy Spirit will lead us into all truth (John 16:13). The problem is, people are impatient with the Holy Spirit, and so they try to give God a hand and speed up the process of change. The reality is this: once you let God into your thoughts and decision making, you will begin to listen and obey His Spirit. He will tell you what is suitable to wear. He will tell you when He feels the timing is best for YOU. This may be two weeks or two years. Although I never fell into the manipulations of not wearing makeup, my attire did change.

I remember wearing revealing clothes when I was not in church, but as my relationship with God grew closer, my attire toned down a little each day until my dress became conservative but still attractive. Again, that was not the work of man; that was the work of the Holy Spirit.

It is important to note one thing. People have the greatest problems with their own problems. Let me explain. If a person spent years in clubs, living a very sinful life, they might have a greater sensitivity to music with a pulsing beat because it reminds them of the club environment. Now the Christian making the music may have been in church their entire life and has no negative associations with the music. This is a small example of how one person can call something sin while the other person has no idea what the problem is.

Some worldly Christians in the church have never let go of old superstitions, religious rules, and ancient customs and have bruised many visitors and members in the church to the point of running them off. They are not spiritually mature and have become religious militants, instead of operating in love and gentleness the way God instructed.

They may think nothing of it after they have wronged or offended you. They do not even know they are making you pay for their old life.

You must pray for these people and keep your distance until God turns them around; you can feed them with words of love and encouragement as long as you don't allow yourself to get hurt in the process.

The Bible tells us to guard our heart above all else, for it determines the course of our life (Proverbs 4:23). I also believe this scripture is telling us to guard our emotions, our mental state, our peace, and anything that could disturb the assurance of God's love for us.

Pastor on the Prowl

I joined a new church a few years after that, with a humble spirit—and I must say, a bit naively—because in my mind I needed to get on a level of excellence that would match the people in this new church. I thought I needed to mature, to become more holy. Now that I'm older and a little wiser, I realize how unrealistic my thinking was. For some reason, I thought these people were better than me. Perhaps that is how you feel about the people in the church, or you may think that's how they want you to feel, but I know now and want you to know that only the blood of Jesus can perfect any of us. Some Christians who make mistakes are very sorry afterwards; they acknowledge their wrong to themselves and to others. They take their actions to God and ask for forgiveness.

However, there are also wolves in sheep's clothing. These individuals walk around with little to no conviction, do not acknowledge their wrongs, and do not repent; they believe that "Jesus died for my sins, so I can do as I please. I am free to sin."

Beware of such a spirit as this. This spirit may be the one who has caused you to veer away from God and question God. I have experienced such a person; it was extremely tough for me because I was a baby Christian who was very trusting at first. One would think if there was anyone in the church who had their head on straight and spirit connected with God, it would be the pastor, right? Wrong! The Bible tells us, "Beware of false prophets who come disguised as harmless sheep but are vicious wolves" (Matthew 7:15).

My spiritual beliefs were challenged when my pastor told me to give him a call about serving as one of the trustees of the church. So I called the office, and the secretary put me on hold to connect the call. I began to pray and prepare myself to properly address the man of God who was over my life. Once we connected, there was a deep, slow "Hello...Shawntá." Not the type of hello you would expect from your pastor. So I said, "Hello, Pastor," and asked him about the committee and my responsibilities. He talked about it briefly and said there were a few questions I had asked him that he was unsure of and wondered if he could call me back. I said okay. He asked if he could call me back tomorrow, and I told him it would not be a good idea because I was going to Jamaica for my birthday. He replied, "How nice—take many pictures, especially in your bikini, and send them to me." I told him I would take lots of pictures, but I would not be sending any in my bikini. He laughed and said he was just teasing.

That vibe I got on the phone was real, and I felt very uncomfortable and was watchful thereafter. About two weeks passed, and I was back home from my vacation. On my first Sunday back in church, I sat next to a girl around my age who was fairly pretty, had a cute shape, and was speaking in tongues, saying over and over "Abba Father," a word of Arabic origin that means "Papa"—describing an affectionate, dependent relationship with your Father God. Although she appeared to be very spiritual, I could sense a bit of distance in her during the service. My discernment about her was brought to light when she asked me for a ride home.

When she got in the car, she started talking about how good the church service was and mentioned that her husband was not in that church, and how she was looking to marry Eddie Long, a famous pastor at New Missionary Baptist Church, a megachurch in Georgia, who, I might add, was married at the time and someone she had never met nor talked to. However, her rants did not stop there. She shared with me the sexual encounters she had indulged in at different churches. It was as if this young lady was pouring out to me how she had been tossed around, used and abused, and spiritually lost, confused, and borderline demonized.

I thought, *God, what is going on in the body of believers? Is my Pastor also responsible for the demise of this young lady? Is this why she was there visiting my church? Is this the norm here? The leadership is killing us spiritually. I must go! I want no part of this.*

In the meantime, the pastor had contacted me through a text message asking me for my birthday pictures, the ones in my bikini, and decided he would start off the sharing by sending me a picture of his genitals. Everything was flooding in all at once; I had enough and decided not to go back to the church.

The only person I confided in was my mother, who could not believe her ears once I shared with her what had happened. She told me not to leave my church but to continue to pray, and God would see to it that the pastor was removed before he harmed any more of His sheep. So after great confusion and much prayer, I went back to the church.

It was extremely hard, trying to listen to the Word and block the true character of the man standing before me, but I did it. Don't get me wrong. Every kind of negative thought about him entered my mind, but one thing this man could do was preach, so my spirit was being renewed and growing. It's funny how I was still gaining spiritual wisdom from a man whose actions were worse than those of most men I came across who wanted nothing to do with God.

I changed my number, did not continue in any ministry but the usher board, prayed faithfully, and that pastor was moved out of my church within six months. Then the revelation came to me that many gifted people make up the body of Christ, from the ministers to the preachers to the pews.

Scripture tells us in Matthew 7:22-23, "Many will say to me in that day, Lord, Lord, have we not prophesied in your name and done many wonders in your name? Moreover, then I will declare to them, I never knew you; depart from me, you who practice lawlessness!"

Jesus also tells the parable of the wheat and the tares in Matthew 13:24-30:

> "The kingdom of heaven is like a man who sowed good seed in his field. However, while everyone was sleeping; his enemy came and sowed weeds among the wheat, and went away. When the wheat sprouted and formed heads, then the weeds also appeared. The owner's servants came to him and said, 'Sir, didn't you sow good seed in your field? Where then did the weeds come from?' 'An enemy did this,' he replied. The servants asked him, 'Do you want us to go and pull them up?' 'No,' he answered, 'because while you are pulling the weeds, you may uproot the wheat with them. Let both grow together until the harvest. 'At that time, I will tell the harvesters: First collect the weeds and tie them in bundles to be burned; then gather the wheat and bring it into my barn.'"

We must stand the test of time in faith as God allows the good and bad people in the body of Christ to grow together.

This is a test of our faith, and God uses our goodness as a testimony to them. We cannot leave the church because God needs true believers to grow and build His kingdom. We have to be the example of God when others are not. God recognizes when you are the wheat and will separate you from the tares and pull you from among them in due time, or else remove them away from you.

However, there are exceptions to staying in a church that exposes too much ungodliness; if you are sexually abused or assaulted and that leader or member is not removed from your church, it is best to report it and leave. Speak up. Suffering abuse in secret is not holy; it is not righteous. It is not of God.

That said, never move out of God's presence, no matter the circumstances, because that is what the devil wants you to do. Remember when I said earlier how the devil can create the environment of holiness? This is what you witness when a leader can preach the walls down yet cannot keep his pants up.

Some alternatives could be to join another church or study and pray at home, but be consistent in your fellowship with God as you seek out another place of worship. The devil constantly works on our leaders to discredit them so that we will not fulfill our destiny in Christ. Don't let him. Remember, God is the best representation of God. Never go to man to check on God. Go to God to check on the man.

During that whole time of my spiritual struggle in dealing with my pastor and questioning whether or not I wanted to leave the church, I was working toward getting a ministry for at-risk girls off the ground. God gave me this ministry, but if I had left His presence and no longer heard the Word of God coming from the pulpit, I may have delayed or abandoned my life assignment. God is so good because even when the devil tries to prostitute the church for his purposes, God still knows how to get His Word through to those who sincerely need to hear a word.

I could have become judgmental and critical. I could have left the church and walked away from the faith altogether. I am so glad I did not.

You also have an assignment—we all do—and you must put on the full armor of God even in the body of believers. Trust me. You will need it. Nothing that God has for you will be easy, but God will equip you to overcome the people in the world and the lost wolves in the body of

Christ and use you as His weapon to win souls and be a true witness and example of who He is.

Situations We Cannot Change

There were just some things in life that I had no control over, such as the death of my best friend, who died from AIDs. We would sit, laugh, and talk about how we would look and walk and talk when we got older. We would stand up and do role-play, arching our backs and shaking our hand like we were holding canes, making jokes and mocking ourselves in the future. When he died, I questioned God's motive because he was the only friend I had who understood me and loved me unconditionally.

He was there for me during my mom's drug addiction and my father's incarceration, and we never had one fight, ever. My questioning God made me begin to doubt if God had a good plan for my life, and in my questioning I could have veered away from God. But I knew in my spirit, after all the grieving, crying, and tantrums, that my friend was free from the pain and suffering and in a better place. Yes, he was saved and a believer in God, so I could rest assured that he was under the wings of God. The Bible says, "All things work together for the good of them that love the Lord and are called according to His purpose" (Romans 8:28). You see, I always loved God, but when I continued to trust fully in Him, He called me into my purpose for His will.

At times I had my questions, just like you may have about the negative events that happen in your life, but with everything that happens, God has a plan for your good. Every storm has to end. It cannot rain all the time. What matters most is whose hand you are holding when the rain clears.

I can promise you, if you decide to hold the hand of God, He will lead you into peace, love, and understanding and minister to your spirit. With every battle, your relationship with God will become stronger after you see all the things He carries you through. You will use your victories as ammunition and hold the scripture in your heart that "No weapon formed against me shall prosper" (Isaiah 54:17).

To be successful in life, you must be around likeminded people to help you achieve, motivate, and sometimes coach you. The same goes for seeking God and the purpose He has for you. You cannot walk the good walk of faith if the people you surround yourself with are not of faith and full of doubt and disbelief.

I remember I met this young man once. We had been dating for a couple of months, and one day I shared with him my dream of taking my Nurturing Hearts students to Africa to embrace their roots and gain a better understanding of their history. After I finished spilling my guts out, his response was, "That will never happen." I immediately pulled over and parked my car. I could not believe my ears. I did not ever want to see his face again, and I told him why. I told him he was a dream killer, and I rebuked every negative spirit that he possessed in the name of Jesus. At that point he probably thought I was crazy as ever, but I did not care.

I knew God had put something deep inside of me, and it would manifest. After I had told him off "in Jesus' name," I sat in the car in disbelief that I had even met someone who would try and put down another person's dreams. About thirty seconds later he called me back and apologized, but at that point I wanted nothing to do with him, period. He told me that when he was a little boy, he would share his dreams with others, and they would tell him all the time that it could not be done.

He said he used that negative energy as fuel to motivate him to do what he dreamed of doing and was looking for my reaction to be the same. I told him how I could never be with a person who shot my dreams down like that, and his tactic almost cost us our relationship. He never did that again. However, imagine if I had said nothing and just let him shoot those negative darts into my spirit. He would have done it all the time and could have potentially killed my dreams.

The devil uses people to shoot fear, doubt, disbelief, and any other negative feeling to get us to veer away from God and our dreams. Recognize the relationships the enemy puts in your life to deter you. Every person you encounter or have a relationship with is either for the purpose of God in your life or against it.

In life, you are always going forward or backward—you are never standing still. But if you must stand still, make sure you are standing still with God. You can discern the spirit by their response to the good things you want to do or happen in your life. However, some are in disguise, and you can see their true face and motive only through prayer and God-given discernment. We will talk about watching and praying in a later chapter.

When We Get in the Way of God

If we are honest with ourselves, it is not just about our upbringing, the people in our lives, the relationships we have, or the situations we face in life that veer us away from God; a lot of the times it can be the face we see in the mirror every day. Sometimes we can play the blame game because in actuality we are afraid to be honest with ourselves, are full of pride or denial, or are so far away from God that we are just too blind to see. I pray that you will be enlightened with your inner truth. Until we are honest with ourselves, we cannot grow, change, and prosper into our destined and divine purpose. Take a moment each day to evaluate yourself, write down your faults, develop goals and steps to get there, and work on them each day.

If you need extra support, go to a pastor or counselor you can trust. Pray that God reveal to you the things you need and the strength to change. Be prepared to be upset and frustrated with the things He reveals to you about yourself, but most importantly, be grateful that He loves you enough to expose those issues and help you to become a better person. This is another gift from God. When we confess our faults, we are asking God to help us instead of trying to cover them up. By doing that, your issues will only get worse and fester, and before you know it they will be out of control, leaving you lost.

Lost Is Not a Stranger to My Soul

It all started in my freshman year of college. College introduces you to different concepts of life: philosophy, free will, different people with different lifestyles. If you are not mature in your faith, with all the options and differences going on around you, you could easily question if what you believe is true. I was a psychology major and loved studying the mind and how it worked, why we think the way we do, our emotions, and all types of theories and hypotheses. This whole new experience, along with the different cultures, religions, and philosophies, left me more open and accepting of individuals into my sacred space. Now don't get me wrong God wants us to love all people but that does not mean we should take on everyone's spirit.

I took down my shield of faith, and that was my biggest mistake. The Bible tells us in Ephesians 6:11-12 to "put on the full armor of God so that you can take your stand against the devil's schemes. For our struggle is not against flesh and blood but against the rulers, against the authorities, against the powers of this dark world and against the spiritual forces of evil in the heavenly realms."

As for me, caught up in all the new experiences that life had to offer, I stopped praying and attending church regularly and started reading more books on different religions, especially the African and voodoo culture. I felt like this was the closest I could get to my native land, and I despised the fact that I did not speak my native language—nor even know what it was for that matter. I was searching for my soul after I had already given it to God, and my actions totally grieved the Holy Spirit.

Are you searching for answers that have already been given to you? I did not realize that every culture has its evils. I had tapped into it and was reading and searching in the darkness where nothing can be found. I had left the godly Christian man I had been engaged to since I was sixteen and fallen in love with a confused spiritual man who had just done seven years in prison for armed robbery. I was missing school, drinking every day, and swirling down a black hole.

The decisions I made cost me my sanity and quickly shifted me into the company of people who did not have my best interests at heart. After being out of the will of God, through all the heaviness and my abandoning God, He still loved me enough to take me back after I had committed adultery with His love. He even gave me a testimony about it so I can help others who have veered out of His will.

You may have veered away from God, but He never veers away from you. HE WILL NEVER LEAVE YOU NOR FORSAKE YOU. Did you know that God is married to the backslider, or the one who has veered away from His love? Jeremiah 3:14 says, "Return, faithless people, declares the LORD, for I am your husband. I will choose one from a town, and two from a clan and bring all to Zion."

If you have veered away, don't worry. God prefers bad people to make a testimony out of their lives. Just look at the life of Moses: he was an alcoholic. Look at the life of King David: he was a whoremonger. And look at the life of the apostle Paul: he was a murderer. Be encouraged, the Lord is asking you to come back home where you belong, to a place that will give you rest, peace, hope, love, and purpose. There is rest in the presence of God, even when things are not going the way you planned. He will still give you peace in times of a storm.

You do not have to go through any struggle alone. God wants to help you through them. Your sins do not keep you from God's love, but they can block your blessings if you do not confess them and ask God for help. He wants to bless you, and He is already aware of your mistakes, but He will never divorce you because He is fully committed to you and me.

 Closing Prayer

Lord, help me to draw close to You. I have veered away and know that I am not where You want me to be. Help me not to reject Your love because of the sins and actions of others; help me to remember that You, and You alone, are perfect. There is nothing I can do to separate Your love from me because Your love is eternal and unconditional. Restore my faith in You. Restore my hope in You. Restore my love in You. I invite You back into my heart, mind, and spirit without hesitation or delay. You said in Your Word that You are married to the backslider, and You said in Your Word that You will never leave or forsake me. Lord, forgive me for falling away and abandoning You. I repent. As I wake each morning, I will give thanks for who You are. You are my King of Kings and Lord of Lords; You are my everything. Thank You for being a Father, a friend, and a helpmate in my time of need. From this day forward, I pray that the Holy Spirit will constantly remind me of Your presence, love, and tender care so that I may forever live in Your presence. In Jesus's name, amen.

Chapter 3

Beware of Your Negative Emotions

We must all manage our negative emotions. We often associate negative emotions with someone upsetting, harming, or taking us for granted, but our worst emotions can be self-inflicted. When we fall short of our plans and dreams, we can be our most critical judge—and our worst enemy.

Fear is one of the most negative emotional reactions we can have because we are reacting negatively to something that may never occur or exist.

The key to leaning in the direction of our positive emotions, as opposed to our negative ones, is mastering and having control over our own emotions, even when other people or situations are out of balance with our inner peace and joy.

Controlling Negative Emotions

The most common negative emotions manifest as anger, anxiety, and fear, whereby we become stubborn within our souls and hinder our own dreams, goals, ambitions, and true selves. As long as we give our negative emotions the upper hand, we cloud our decision making and creative capacity.

For instance, we can let a failed relationship slow us down and stop us from having future loving, lasting, strong relationships because of the emotions yet to be healed.

It is imperative to heal properly from a broken heart, disappointments, and setbacks, and we must take responsibility and work on improving ourselves when situations and people attack our emotions. We must remain conscious and stable, pushing through our emotions like a football player breaking through his opponents to make a touchdown.

Let's continue to think positive, believe we can move on, think we have what it takes, and be persuaded that we can be and do all that we set out to achieve by staying on the high path. Make a choice to proactively develop and maintain a healthy mind, body, and spirit.

If we want to achieve a life full of joy and peace, we must know there is a season for everything and understand that no season stays the same. We have the power to change our winter into spring!

Our power is our choice. We must go beyond our emotions by analyzing and searching deeply within our thoughts with the primary goal of thinking clearly, making the right decisions, and knowing that we can overcome any obstacle, any circumstance, or any person standing in our way.

This can only be achieved by learning and speaking positive affirmations to ourselves—accompanied with Scripture—and thinking before we act out our negative responses. Yes, we may cry, but we must think through our tears, meditate, and pray for solutions to our problems. Let's be as dedicated to finding healthy remedies for our pain as we are in focusing on the results from the harmful event. In other words, as much energy as you put into feeling bad about whatever happened to you, place that same amount of energy and time determining to be happy, whole, and fulfilled.

Physics is not just for scientists; it is for happiness. We all studied Newton's third law of motion in high school: "For every action, there is an equal and opposite reaction." The problem is this: many times we allow one-sided actions to hijack our lives. When someone hurts us, we live in that hurt, not realizing there is an opposite action available to us. For every hurt, grab ahold of joy; for every tear, grab ahold of laughter; for every disappointment, grab ahold of encouragement. Don't wait— grab ahold of the opposite side of your negative emotions today!

We all have two emotional elements raging inside of us for control: our inner enemy and our inner friend. Our inner enemy is the one who probes us to worry, lash out, and remain in doubt, fear, and anger. Our inner friend is cheering for us to remain peaceful, full of joy, stress-free, prosperous, and capable of positive solutions and growth. Whomever we listen to determines how successful we will become in life.

Beware of people who manipulate your emotions by taking advantage of your weaknesses, fears, or anxieties. These may be friends, relatives, and loved ones who are wolves dressed in sheep's clothing. The worst wolves are those who are not even aware they are wolves.

Many people have been so conditioned to be negative they do it automatically. Without intent to do you harm, these people can harm you by their very nature. Be watchful and pray for discernment to know who is speaking to you. More important than the words someone says to you are the words you say to yourself. Speak positively to yourself; remove those self-doubting thoughts that come from within you and from the opinions of others.

Embrace your inner friend and let it arise within you; give yourself compliments and direction. Tell yourself, "I am good enough, I have what it takes, I will succeed, I am strong enough, and I can make it." Relax in that still, small voice letting you know you can do all things through Christ who strengthens you, and live your life to the fullest in spite of your inner enemy. Negative feelings and emotions do not have to take control of you. Instead, learn to move through your negative feelings and emotions to change your life for the better, accepting your God-given gifts of happiness, prosperity, wealth, emotional stability, and peace, and bringing the life you dream of to fruition.

Emotions can be your friend or your worst enemy

Learning to control your impulses and emotions is a sign of wisdom and maturity, leading you down the path of purpose, happiness, and spiritual growth. This mindset allows you to learn from your mistakes and serves as a catalyst for growth, warning you when change or removal from a situation, activity, or person is needed in your life.

If we are not sensitive to the voice of God and do not allow Him to implant wisdom inside of us, these emotions can trigger responses that will do the exact opposite of what we need.

The Bible states that when I was a child, I spoke as a child and did as a child. If we cannot control our emotions and let other people's actions influence *our* actions, then we are like children going along in life doing what our feelings force us to do. As we become older, we believe that with maturity comes self-control, discipline, and the fruits of the spirit: love, joy, peace, patience, kindness, goodness, faithfulness, gentleness, and self-control.

Au contraire, my friend. There is a song by the late singer Aaliyah called "Age Ain't Nothing But a Number." The song is about her maturity level, which she believed had very little to do with her young age (I believe she was only sixteen at the time). Now, let's be clear, when this song was out, I did believe that age was nothing but a number. What sixteen-year-old doesn't? However, in truth, older individuals also use this belief, but in reverse. They too believe that age is just a number, and because they have been on the earth for forty years or more, they think they are mature. Some may even believe that because they were born and raised in the church all their lives, they are spiritually mature.

Do not be deceived. The length of time you have been doing something has nothing to do with maturity. In fact, it could very well mean you've been doing something wrong for a long time! Romans 12:3 says, "Do not think of yourself more highly than you ought to, but rather think of yourself with sober judgment, by the faith God has distributed to each of you." If any of you has ever had a little too much to drink, your judgment about yourself and others is clouded. You make unwise decisions and could end up doing some pretty stupid things. We have all witnessed someone making an idiot of themselves at the expense of celebrating too hard with alcohol. Just as someone is drunk through alcohol, when we think too highly of ourselves, we become drunk with pride. We deceive ourselves. Therefore, it is very important for us to do "self-assessments." This is where we sit down and make a list of all the responsibilities we have in life, such as work, school, family, and marriage.

Ask yourself: Okay, I am older, but how am I wiser minus my age, and where am I still immature? How do I see my children, career, relationship, and lifestyle choices? My finances, temper, judging of others, spiritual growth, restoring relationships, inner peace, and emotional wellbeing?

You may have a few more items you would like to add to the list. Write the headings down, underline them, and under each write down some goals to make each item better. The key to succeeding at this is taking a moment to ponder each category individually, being totally honest with yourself and your inner soul. After you have completed your list, ask yourself, "Where am I in my life on this subject? Where do I want to be? What are some steps I can take to get there?" Schedule a day of the week to work on each one, or you may have time to pick hours throughout the day to work on them. Pray over it each day, monitor your progress, and watch yourself begin to grow. You may want to reach out to someone you trust who can share this journey of growth and maturity, to walk with and encourage one another.

We can change our negative emotions by simply growing up. It is not really how others treat us, but how we respond that reflects our maturity and emotional stability. Anger, resentment, gossip, backstabbing—anyone at any age can respond in that manner; it's easy and expected by most people in the world. I challenge you to do the unexpected and bless those who curse you, forgive those who harm you, ignore those who try to manipulate you. Be confident that you still have the ultimate weapon of warfare: prayer. God is always fighting on our behalf. Romans 12:19 says: "Do not take revenge, my dear friends, but leave room for God's wrath, for it is written: 'It is mine to avenge; I will repay,' says the Lord."

I can attest that when the Lord says He will take revenge on the person who wronged you, He means it. There is a lesson that God must teach them, and usually it will involve suffering until they humble themselves under the mighty hand of God. The less you interfere with God's plans, the better.

I know what it's like to feel the emotions of pain, anger, and sadness through the betrayal of a close friend and ex-boyfriend whom I still loved dearly during the time of betrayal. I had to make the wise decision to let go of an unhealthy relationship, which is an emotional experience all by itself.

It was the Fourth of July, the sky was sunny, and I was at peace with my decision to end the relationship; I had begun to heal and move on. As I was leaving a store, I saw a man driving down the street, music blasting, windows down, smiling, laughing, and bobbing his head. It was my ex and my so-called girlfriend. I tried to play it cool even though I was as hot as the devil's lake of fire. I gave a piercing glance to make sure my eyes had not deceived me and proceeded to walk to my car.

However, they wanted to be seen and wanted me to see them. They laughed and waved at me. Yep, they waved at me. I kept my cool, but within it felt like fiery darts hitting every nerve inside my body. I wanted to be like those cartoons where the characters send a bomb from far away in the distance. Then you just see a cloud of smoke as the bomb hits its target. That would have been soooo nice… However, I know, we are supposed to manage negative emotions.

I carried on to my mom's house to take her the bag of charcoal and drinks. I went outside to start the grill, and as I tried to light it my hand trembled, I was so full of anger. Although I was very quiet on the outside, the anger was showing its ugly head in my actions. My mind flooded with thoughts about hurting my friend, beating her up, or paying someone else to do it; I thought of multiple ways to hurt them both. I left the grill unlit, went into my mother's room alone, and cried in anger and sadness. I prayed and asked God to calm me down; it took a while, but I did. Then the Holy Spirit began to minister to me saying, "I am the revenge. We both saw that their purpose was to harm you deliberately. Don't worry, I got this."

At that very moment, I released them and put them both in the hands of God, knowing that what I had with my ex would never be able to be fixed because he was unwilling to change. The girl I thought was my friend, well, her character was being revealed to protect me from future pain. I was blessed that God exposed the two of them so that I could have only the people He wanted for me in this life.

This is why we have to control our emotions. Do you see how God was able to minister to me after I calmed down? We must not let our emotions overtake us, because it is difficult to let God's wisdom into our ears and hearts (something we need most when we are going through a crisis) when we are not quiet enough to listen to His instructions. Unfortunately, today my former friend is heavily on drugs, and my ex has been in and out of jail every few years. Although God is working on both of them, my heart is never in the place to see anyone hurt. I still pray for the both of them.

Once I got over my pain, let go, and let God manage it, I came to the realization that the only reason they were looking to hurt me was because they both were lost and hurting themselves. Remember, it is not always just about you, so stay strong and stay with God. Don't let your emotions overtake you, and let Him work things out for your good. It will save you much fear, strife, trouble, pain, and anxiety. Rest assured, He is your Best Friend.

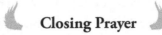

Closing Prayer

O Lord, help me to overcome my emotions and rest in Your presence of peace. Whatever I am feeling, allow me to trust You more than this emotion, knowing there is nothing that I cannot get through when I cast my cares upon You. Help me to rest in You, believe in You, and put all my trust in You. I will not be quick to anger. I will not be quick to fear. I will not allow jealousy or sadness to overtake me. I will acknowledge my emotion but then immediately give it to You. I trust that all things are working out in my favor, and I know that nothing happens that You have not allowed. You said in Your Word that all things work together for the good to them that love the Lord and are called according to His purpose. Lord, no matter what is going on in my life right now, I know that I am called according to Your purpose, and You have peace, love, and joy on the other side of my struggle. As I pray and wait patiently, I receive and thank You in advance for everything good coming my way. In Jesus's name, amen.

Chapter 4

The Art of Forgiveness
and the Power Within

David and I sat down over a cappuccino to talk. He was interested in hearing about a presentation I was doing on forgiveness at the women's hospital. I told him how I had not fully forgiven my mother for using drugs until I was in my early twenties. My mother was an awesome mom before her addiction. I remember her coming home from work with her briefcase and buying me Barbie dolls every Friday when she got paid. She would go skating with me and my friends and have cool talks with me in the evening about how fun it is being a girl and how young ladies should carry themselves with respect.

Sadly, all of that changed after my parents got a divorce. My mom and I moved out into the projects and her friends began to change.

My mother owned a modeling agency, but after the move that fell between the cracks. No longer did her business partners and models come to visit; now her friends consisted of drugs dealers, drug addicts, and alcoholics, and it wasn't long before my mother became addicted to crack cocaine herself.

It broke my heart to see her suffer like that every day. Crack addicts and drugs dealers came in and out of our house from morning until night, sometimes overnight. I often woke up to the smell of crack cocaine seeping from under the bathroom door as I got my little brother ready for school. I would go to school in a silent pain that showed up through fights I refused to walk away from. From the time I was nine until eighteen I saw too much in a place that was supposed to be safe and filled with love.

Soon David opened up to share his childhood story with me. We both grew up in the projects and had pretty rough childhoods. However, David's upbringing was a lot worse than mine. Sometimes we may think our story is bad; we may complain about having no shoes until we meet a man with no feet.

David told me that he was adopted at the age of five. His mother was on crack cocaine and involved in the dangerous world of prostitution. Because of this, David was sent to foster care and adopted by women who abused him mentally and physically. These women would say things like, "You are nothing and ain't never going to be nothing. You are going to grow up to be just like your mother: a drug addict and a loser." His foster mothers sometimes beat him until he bled, leaving cuts on his legs and arms. They would make him take hot baths, causing the wounds to sting. David, now in his forties, wept as he recalled the acts of violence aimed at him at such a young age.

As I listened to his story I thought, *My mother put me through a lot, but she never gave up on me. She didn't leave me or abuse me. She really did the best she could while in her illness.* There is a song by the late Tupac

Shakur called "Dear Mama," written about his mother, who was also on crack like mine was. Whenever I heard it as a young girl, I always related to the lyrics.

I reached out, squeezing both his hands, and apologized for what he had suffered at the hands of abusers posing as loving mothers. Then I asked him if he could find it in his heart to forgive them. He smiled and said, "Yes." I wiped my eyes and asked how.

David gave me four answers that were also the same reasons why I had forgiven my mother for using drugs and not being the mother I needed while growing up. The same four reasons I used to forgive my father for not being in my life. The first reason was that the burden to hang onto something was too heavy. The weight of unforgiveness ultimately crushes the one holding onto it. Unforgiveness prevents us from moving forward. Unforgiveness prevents us from accomplishing our dreams, enjoying day-to-day life, and embracing love, peace, and happiness.

Second, he said he was aware of his failure in relationships and started to backtrack down the road that had led him straight to his unforgiveness. This was so interesting because I remember David in middle and high school. He was a heartbreaker, very attractive, but the way he treated girls sucked. David would treat women like toys on Christmas Day: loved you and played with you today, but wouldn't speak to you or touch you tomorrow. I remember he liked this pretty cheerleader in high school. He chased her for about three months, and she finally went out on a date with him. During the date, he told me, he made a mental list of all her flaws and things she did wrong. The next day in school, he spread all these dirty rumors about her, lied to her, and talked about her like she was nothing.

David would cheat on girls and physically abuse them. It was not until he forgave and sought counseling and a true relationship with God that he was able to have successful, loving, fruitful relationships.

He has now been happily married for five years and has two beautiful children. I believe David would never have had a great family structure and success had he not forgiven those who wronged him. I am sure he would have had tons of baby mamas and children who felt abandoned as he did as a child, but his forgiveness reversed the curse and instead activated blessings.

This brings me to the third reason David said he decided to forgive. He said unforgiveness was like a curse he was passing on to other people he was in a relationship with, like a terrible flu. You see, when negative things happen to us, or if we do something that harms another person, we must repent so that these spirits do not stay alive. When we do not forgive, we are not releasing those experiences but holding onto them until they become a part of who we are.

Because of this, you see people all over the world who have been abused and become an abuser, who have been raped and become a child molester, who were abandoned and feel it is okay to abandon their children. Yes, the wrong done to us was meant to destroy our lives, our relationships, and our destiny in God. However, we have the power to stop it. We have a choice and a God who is ready to take on all our cares, for Matthew 11:28-30 (KJV) says, "Come unto me, all ye that labor and are heavy-laden, and I will give you rest. Take my yoke upon you and learn from me; for I am meek and lowly in heart, and ye shall find rest unto your souls. For my yoke is easy and my burden is light."

What are you holding onto that is a burden in your life? When you think about it as a curse or a disease, it should change how you look at what you are carrying and doing to yourself. Unforgiveness is a burden, a weight, a hindrance, with the ability and goal to take you out. Take you out of joy, love, peace, purpose, and blessings.

How do you see forgiveness? Most people never forgive because their fundamental perception or belief about forgiveness is all wrong. You may think forgiveness is letting the other person win, or being weak and vulnerable, or letting someone take advantage of you again, but forgiveness is none of the above.

Psychologists define forgiveness as a conscious, deliberate decision to release feelings of resentment or vengeance toward a person or group who has harmed you, regardless of whether they deserve your forgiveness.

One word stuck out to me in this definition, and that word is "deserve"—worthy of being treated a particular way. I want you to look deep within your soul and think about all the things you have done or even thought about doing that you know are not pleasing to God. Now think to yourself, what would your life be like if you truly got what you deserved? Scary right?

Forgiveness is a gift we give ourselves. It allows us to heal, gives us inner peace, and helps us to grow into our best selves: in our minds, bodies, and spirits.

Unforgiveness can also cause sickness and depression within our bodies and minds because we are releasing toxins and chemicals that we are not consciously aware of. Not releasing the harmful emotion of unforgiveness affects our health, causing cancer, diseases, and possible death. We can develop ulcers, body aches, and a compromised immune system. How we think determines how we feel, and how we feel determines how we behave, so if we are pondering our failures, mishaps, and abuse, soon we will become the very situation that happened to us. Don't let one situation control your life. It is so much more to you than what you have experienced.

You can turn your pain into power by healing and saving someone else who is going through the same things you went through. Become a conqueror, and take control of your hurt so you can be free to share your story, to heal and uplift others as I have chosen to do. This is the only way to win. The devil wants you to repress those feeling of abuse because he knows if you confront them, you will be so much more powerful as an overcomer than as a sad victim. When you rise above your pain and decide to live a happy, prosperous life, you confuse the person who harmed you. You disarm the spirit that haunts you with the pain. Our mind is a battlefield, because what we think about, meditate on, and hide within our subconscious is what we give power to, and that in turn affects our day-to-day lives.

According to James chapter 3, if you harbor bitter envy and contention/selfish ambition in your heart, you will find disorder and every evil practice.

Ultimately, people who refuse to forgive hurt themselves. People who hold grudges do not make good friends or company. They cannot sleep well. They see the negative in every situation because their life is filled with these feelings of hatred and anger. People who are unwilling to forgive may feel they are making the other person suffer, but the only person dying inside is themselves.

How do you begin to forgive?

We can begin to forgive by discovering the person who hurt us and acknowledging their illness. Yes, the person who wronged you had some serious issues, some of which may have been easy to see while others were hidden by sarcasm and false pride. Of course, you were hurt, and I am not downplaying that, but I want you to understand the depth of your pain and where it originated from, because I can almost guarantee it did not start with you. In fact, it had very little to do with you.

Think of a person who's wronged you as you would a homeless person: poor, dirty, needy, perhaps smelly and lost. When we see the homeless, we know nothing about them. They could have abused a wife, mother, or friend; they could be a con artist. They could have just been released from jail for committing a vicious crime, but in spite of us knowing nothing about them, we give them money. We build homeless shelters and soup kitchens for them. Why do we do this? Well, most of the time we feel sorry for them, we have pity for them, and when we give them a few dollars we feel as if we are doing a good deed. We feel the Lord will be pleased with us, right?

What if I told you that the person who wronged you was just like the homeless? Not homeless, lacking food or shelter, but homeless in his/her spirit, emotions, thoughts, and behavior? There's a well-known saying that "hurt people hurt people." I can almost guarantee that the person who did you wrong had some form of "homelessness." Maybe it was alcohol, drug abuse, or mental disability; perhaps they were abused as a child. So as an adult they don't know how to love. Something in their life was out of place that caused them to act in such a way. Take a moment and think about what their homelessness may have been. You will find someone full of confusion, low self-esteem, and pain. Forgive them.

After you have looked at your abuser through the spiritual eyes of truth, you can then prepare yourself to surrender your right to revenge. When we seek revenge, we place ourselves in the spirit of wrongdoing that makes us just as bad as the person who hurt us. We become our own abuser by letting them control our response.

Recognize the homelessness in them, and understand that if you respond with a vengeful spirit you keep the curse alive. This will allow you to change the way you think and feel toward the person you forgive. When we do not forgive, we give that person power to rule over a part of our life by taking up space in our mind, space that can be used for our God-designed destiny. He does not give us the desires of our hearts and answers to our prayers if we allow hate, resentment, and vengeance to block our relationship with Him. James 3:14-16 says that if we have bitter envy and self-seeking in our hearts, this "wisdom" is not from above and every type of evil will come from these feelings.

As I travel through life, I have realized that if the enemy cannot get us to walk away from God, he will try the next best thing by encouraging us not to forgive. He knows unforgiveness hinders our prayers and therefore affects our relationship with God. David the psalmist wrote, "If I regard iniquity in my heart the Lord will not hear" (Psalm 66:18). If God does not hear our prayers, our prayers are hindered. If God does not hear when we pray, we pray without power.

We have to stop thinking that we are doing the person who wronged us an awesome favor by forgiving them. Forgiveness is a gift we give ourselves, allowing us to heal emotionally, physically, and spiritually.

Forgiveness Does Not Mean Relationship

Forgiveness usually includes reconciliation (a restored relationship). Why? The standard for our forgiveness of others is God's forgiveness of us. As Col.3:13 says, "Bear with each other and forgive one another if any of you has a grievance against someone. Forgive as the Lord forgave you." When God forgives us, He does not in essence say, "Okay, now go on with your life, we're good." No, He forgives us and reconciles with us (i.e., brings us into a restored relationship with Him). Our human forgiveness of others is to reflect that kind of forgiveness, as much as it is possible and as wisdom dictates.

But we also have to show caution with abusive people we forgive. This is wise. Yes, forgiveness includes reconciliation in our human relationships, but reconciliation does not look the same in every relationship. For people who have hurt you repeatedly or physically or sexually abused you, it is extremely unwise to reconcile with them like you would a normal friend or family member with whom you had a falling out. Know that forgiveness does not mean "Hurt me again." When we forgive, we are deciding to heal. You can forgive someone who is not even sorry and refuses to change, because forgiveness does not always come with restoring a relationship. Forgiveness is about restoring your broken soul. Reconciliation with an abuser can and probably should be something like this: "We are at peace and I forgive you" Period. I would NOT recommend spending time with that person, normalizing a relationship, or at a minimum, spending time alone with them. I think in that case, you have met the biblical definition of forgiveness. Remember, with "normal" offenses, reconciliation looks different.

But for hard cases of forgiveness and hurt, you do not, nor should you, have to walk in this alone. Seek the wisdom of a godly pastor or counselor. There are skilled and loving people to come along side you and help you make good decisions and give you support. That's what they are there for and even if it's hard, asking for help is often a first, brave step in the process."

In my presentations, I like to use an egg demonstration to explain the difference between these two options. Two volunteers come up, and I give each of them an egg. I ask volunteer one to drop the egg. When they drop the egg, it breaks and splashes everywhere. This is an example of someone who has hurt you and is unwilling to fix the situation. There is no putting the egg back together. The shell has mixed in the egg, and you cannot fry it because it is dirty. Now, you could become vengeful and pick up what is left of the egg, throwing it against the wall and at others around you. This only causes a bigger mess. Or you could get some paper towels, clean it up, cry a little, throw it away, and let it go.

Next, volunteer two drops the egg, but it does not break; however, the shell is cracked. This is an example of someone who has hurt you but is sorry and willing to change. I begin unpeeling the hardboiled egg, and each piece of shell I remove represents your abuser fixing and working on something about themselves. They have apologized and are seeking counseling. You start to see improvement, and before you know it all of the cracked shell is gone. All you have left is a smooth, soft egg. God restores your relationship in this example, but as you can see it takes work. However, restoring a relationship back to love is worth it.

I thank God for the friendship my parents and I now have. I could have missed out if I did not let go of my ego and pride. I grieve inside when I hear young adults talk badly about parents who abandoned them as children. I think to myself, "You could heal and have peace if you would let go of the grudge and forgive." If you have a parent who was not able to love you in the past for whatever reason, forgive and accept the love they have for you now. They may have been homeless when they had you.

My mother lost her father, married mine (who was abusive), then suffered from depression and drug addiction. Today she is my prayer warrior and the most supportive, funny, and loving mother in the entire world. My father was a thug who decided to let the streets and the judicial system raise him. He said he was a street soldier. Now he is a proud father whom I share jokes and laugh with every week. He calls me almost every day. These relationships would not have been restored if I did not acknowledge their homelessness, human mistakes, and forgive. Could you be missing out on someone who is willing to restore a relationship? If so you can experience this same love that I experience. Don't cheat yourself. Don't let the devil rob you of the joy you deserve. God is waiting to turn that pain into pleasure, but you must take the first step and forgive.

Here is an exercise I do with my class: take a piece of paper and write down the name of the person who harmed you, and then write down the homelessness of that person. Were they on drugs, mentally ill, abused, and/or alcoholic? Think very hard because something is there. Meditate on their homeless state and recite:

- I forgive you. I see the homelessness in you. Therefore, I seek no vengeance.
- I wish you well.
- I know that forgiving you is a gift I owe myself that will allow me to heal.

- I am releasing you into the hands of God and healing now.
- God is healing me.
- I am free to be happy and experience love on all levels.

Closing Prayer

O Lord, give me the strength to let go of this pain deep down inside of me. I want to be free from the torment of [FILL IN NAME] within my thoughts. I refuse to give them power over me because of what they have done. From this day forward, I have no chains binding me. I forgive [NAME] in the name of Jesus. I will no longer be a prisoner of hate and revenge; instead, I ask You to replace them with an inner love and peace within my soul. Lay on me a forgiving spirit. Help me to identify the homelessness in [NAME] and pray for their weakness and illness. As I go through this process, I believe every day I will be healing myself, growing in my spirit, and opening a window of blessings that has been jammed for a very long time because of my unforgiveness. Lord, I pray that every blessing I blocked because of my pain and hatred will be released unto me in the name of Jesus. Fill any void that has been caused by my pain; flood me with Your strength and love. I forgive because You forgave me for my sins, and I want to continue to walk in Your blessings and love. I am free. In Jesus's name, amen.

Chapter 5

Sowing and Reaping

L ove is the strongest act. God so loved the world that He gave His only begotten Son. Some loving relationships can leave you in a spell of passion, neglecting all others. Once you're shot with Cupid's arrow, nothing else matters. Love is to be cherished, appreciated, respected, and dedicated, among other positive things, but most importantly given back in return. However, not everyone feels the same way about love. There are those who take advantage, manipulate, misguide, hurt, and lead others on for their selfish or devilish satisfaction.

A married couple who lived in our neighborhood when I was a young girl appeared to be the perfect couple. They both dressed nice, always smiling, and waved to me from across the street, but that was all a mask because a couple times a week, while the husband was at work, I would watch from my living room window as random men came in and out of their house. It was obvious she was having multiple affairs behind his back. From what I could see, this man loved this woman and would do just about anything for her. She always had nice jewelry, the latest handbags, and new outfits. He would open the car door for her, but it just wasn't enough. This went on for years. I even overheard them arguing and him yelling, "Why...why, just why!"

He would sit in the driveway in his red Mercedes-Benz sometimes for hours. I think he was crying in there. It had been at least six months, and there was no sign of her. A rumor claimed that she had left him for an older man who was physically abusing her. About five years later, I saw her on a street known for heavy drug pushing and prostitution, walking up and down the block wearing a hot pink mini dress, white thigh-high boots, and hot pink lipstick, with a bruised right eye. She had succumbed to selling her body for money.

I felt really bad for her, so I tooted the horn. She looked as if she was trying to figure out who I was, or if I was a client. She ran up to the car; I rolled down my window. I could tell by her covered-up smile that she recognized me and was a little embarrassed. I gave her $20 and said, "God still loves you."

"Are you sure?" she said.

"Of course I am," I replied. "There is nothing so bad that He cannot fix."

As I drove off, I couldn't help but think about how she messed up a good relationship and was reaping what she had sown. Now it was between her and God. I prayed that God would have mercy on her and that she would be free from her sins and the pain she was experiencing.

When you hear the phrase "reaping and sowing," most of us think about giving tithes to a church. The phrase is usually followed by the preacher saying what we give shall be given back to us, pressed down, shaken together, and running over. However, reaping and sowing is not just about using your faith to gain wealth or material things. Reaping and sowing is also every word, every deed, and every thought that we put into existence.

Whatever you release into yourself—into your spirit, into your thoughts—you will reap that back. Whatever you plant into someone else's life—into their spirit, into their thoughts, even into their ears—you will get that back. Whatever you release into the world has a way of coming back to you. It is not just about tangible things; it is not just about money. This is why we have to be very careful how we treat others, how we speak to one another, and how we care or not care for others, because our intentions for others have a way of becoming our reality.

Thinking Positive Thoughts

We want to think positive thoughts because when we meditate on positive thoughts we are planting mental seeds. What you think determines how you feel, and how you feel determines how you will behave. What you meditate on is a seed. How you allow yourself to feel cultivates that seed. How you behave is the harvest that your thought produces. This is why it is crucial to think positive thoughts and meditate on the Word of God. Meditate upon the Word day and night. His Word is the greatest fertilizer for a successful life.

Sowing into Other People's Lives

Sowing into other people's lives is vital. Some of the happiest people on earth are givers, because not only do they give financially, but they give of themselves, helping to build up others. As they give, they receive something back within their spirit. I can attest to this, having founded a nonprofit organization for at-risk girls, going to group homes and foster care units, speaking into the lives of broken and misguided youth. There is a joy unspeakable as I share love, joy, and wisdom with these girls. At times it gets a little tiring and challenging, but once fatigue is gone, joy takes its place and rejuvenates me. I know the seeds I planted in them will spring up as a rich harvest in their lives one day. It is going to be something positive that will help them to grow.

In turn, I can feel the Lord is pleased with me. I know in my heart that as I help them, He will also take care of me. We cannot out-give God, no matter how hard we try. If you give a smile to someone who may be feeling down, God could send a person your way to bless you with a gift. Perhaps you said some encouraging words to someone at work. In turn, God could put an awesome teacher in your child's path who puts in the extra time when he/she needs it.

I remember standing in line at Subway one time and this older white lady, with pretty flowers in her hair and a bubbly personality, was in front of me getting ready to pay for her sub. I asked her if I could bless her and pay for her meal. She smiled, leaned toward me, and whispered, "Why certainly, pretty lady. I see you know one of the greatest secrets in life." She patted my arm and said, "Double." I immediately knew she operated in the spirit of giving and receiving. She was enlightening just as I was. About two days later, I received a lump sum of money for my nonprofit organization. I gave $7 and some change from the kindness of my heart and reaped a donation large enough to sustain my organization for an entire year. I sowed a seed from the goodness of my heart and reaped a great harvest.

It has been said that there is good and bad karma. When we do good to others, it comes back to us. The same is true when we mistreat others. When we have done wrong unto others, many of us will say, "Well, I'll just repent and everything will be all right." That could not be further from the truth. We can repent and ask God to forgive us, and He will because He is a forgiving God, but it does not take away the consequences. The consequence of a broken relationship with someone, if not repaired or restored, can make life more difficult.

This is similar to free will and sin. We all have free will and can do whatever we want to do. Our God is a gentleman and will not control us, but when we sin, such as stealing, lying, and cheating, there are consequences. These can all have consequences such as jail, broken hearts, and failed relationships. God forgives us, but if we break the law we will be sitting behind bars in God's grace, mercy, and forgiveness. Be mindful daily of how you respond to people, how you respect people, how you make other people feel. How you make others feel is very powerful because you are releasing vibrations into the atmosphere that have the ability to come back to you.

Proverbs 13:2 tells us that a man shall eat well by the fruit of *his* mouth. The Bible also teaches us that blessing and curses should not come out of the same mouth. I believe that if you are blessed but releasing curses, it defiles and dilutes your spirit. If you are a believer, God is living inside of you, but His marvelous light does not want to remain where you allow hatred to grow and bring people's spirits down.

If you have harmed someone, disappointed someone, or hurt someone, there is a way to make it right. First, repent to God, asking Him for forgiveness. Second, ask that person for forgiveness. Third, forgive yourself. Forgiving ourselves when we have wronged someone is really important because when we can forgive ourselves, we can let go of the weight holding us down. The guilt holding us back can kill us by causing stress, which leads to disease, and depression. When we forgive ourselves, we release all of that from manifesting in our bodies and spirits. It is no longer attached to our life, sucking out our joy and happiness. We can continue to grow, love, and be loved freely.

Some of the people we have hurt and disappointed may refuse to accept our forgiveness. Back in high school, I started dating a guy when I was around fifteen, and we got engaged a year later. We stayed in the relationship until I was about eighteen. That relationship was unsuccessful because I was not prepared for marriage or a serious relationship at such a young age. I could not find the right words to tell him that I was not interested in a relationship. Instead, I just stayed, and by doing so I led him on and broke his heart badly.

Years later, after we both became adults, I decided to reach out to him to apologize and explain how young, stupid, and immature I was, but he refused to accept my apology. He refused to respond to my messages. I could have sulked in my guilt and continued into despair, but instead I chose to move on with my life. I asked God for forgiveness, dug up the bad seed by going to him and apologizing, forgave myself, and continued to grow. He did not receive the new seed I had planted. He chose to let that dead seed take root in him and fester.

What I had done was now clearly off my conscious. I had to humble myself in front of God. When we humble ourselves, it reveals our best self. Many people have to fall in order to see clearly what is up above. Some have to lie on the ground on their backs just to get a full appreciation of what is above: the sun, the moon, the stars—all the Lord has to offer, His great gifts to His children.

So humbling yourself is not a bad thing, although people try to make it out to be a negative trait, as if you are belittling yourself or stepping off a throne. Only God sits on the throne, and He was willing to humble Himself even unto the death of the cross. Jesus being the King of Kings and Lord of Lords had to humble Himself and be beaten and abused until He was eventually killed, but He rose again with power in His hands. That is exactly how I feel when I've humbled myself and asked for forgiveness. I get up with the power of thinking and acting as God thought and acted.

By going back and planting good seeds, I am releasing the person who offended me or who I offended, and I am releasing myself into a spiritual awakening where the Holy Spirit can use me and take me to the place where eyes have not seen, nor ears heard. A place He has prepared for me. But I must clear the path and begin on the right ground.

If you have planted bad seeds in the lives of others, or planted bad seeds in your own life, know that it is never too late to replant. We are human, we all make mistakes; we all say things we should not say, think things we should not think, do things we should not do. As long as we are still blessed to be alive and on this earth, God is giving us another chance to make it right with others and with ourselves. So I challenge you to find that bad seed—and it may not be very hard to find. It may be in yourself. I want you to go back to that place and find where that seed was buried. I want you to dig it up with repentance, dig it up with forgiveness, dig it up knowing that you do not have to dig it up by yourself. The Lord will help you, and He is always ready for reconciliation. He is always ready to make whatever went wrong, right. All we have to do is ask Him to help us. He has the love that no one else may have for you called unconditional love. No matter what you have done to yourself, and no matter what you have done to others, God is always there, waiting for you to ask for forgiveness.

He will go with you if you are afraid to ask someone for forgiveness or afraid to look yourself in the mirror. You do not have to face whatever it is alone. The Holy Spirit is waiting to help you. The Bible calls Him your helpmate and counselor. So ask Him right now, this very moment, to help you go back and dig up what you buried. There is no seed too deep for God; there is no root too strong. God can uproot anything in your heart that does not belong to Him. He can give you a clean heart if you ask Him for it. You have to be willing to believe, and He will take whatever is wrong and make it right.

Nothing has to stay the same; you do not have to walk around in unhealthy relationships with people. There are so many testimonies of restored relationships, restored lives, and restored people. Go ahead and decide to go back to that seed. Dig it out and replace it with the seed of God and new actions of a better, wiser, and loving you. That will cause you not to plant seeds like that ever again. You will begin to think before you plant a seed and instead plant seeds of love, joy, peace, encouragement, faith, kindness, and giving without wanting anything in return. But God will see your heart and reward you for what you have done.

If we use our tongue to kill others (Proverbs 12:19), we ultimately destroy our own spirit. Don't live that way; choose to live by the love that God wants to plant inside each and every one of our hearts.

Your harvest is waiting for you. When it comes up, let it be a harvest that pushes you into your destiny, into your purpose, into the will of God, so that you might receive the crown of crowns from the ultimate King of Kings and Lord of Lords. You are a King's kid, and He has riches stored up that He wants to release to you. You can only receive them if you sow good seed.

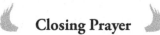

Closing Prayer

Father, forgive me for any harm I may have caused others or myself. Show me how to take the best care of my body, mind, and spirit. I know my body is Your temple, so help me keep it pure and holy for Your dwelling. Remove any selfish, disrespectful, or inconsiderate ways I may have; pull them out by their roots. Give me a clean heart, one that radiates love through and through. If I have wronged someone, give me a humble spirit so that I may apologize and make it right between that person and me, but most importantly, make my relationship right with You. Instill within me the fruits of the Spirit: love, joy, peace, patience, kindness, goodness, faithfulness, gentleness, and self-control. Let me be a light of joy to others and for myself. Let my actions, words, thoughts, and deeds reflect You. In Jesus's name, amen.

Chapter 6

Watch and Pray

P rayer is oxygen. Without it we die. Matthew 26:41 tells us to "watch as well as pray." I believe when we watch and pray, we not only watch with our eyes but also with our hearts, with guidance from the Holy Spirit. It is very important to apply this scripture and godly instruction throughout life's journey because many times we think it is enough to pray simply. I have said one-word prayers that only included one name, "Jesus," because that was all I had the strength to say at the time, and the Lord heard, acknowledged, and answered my prayer. He knows my heart and is faithful. He even knows the heart of our heart. That is, He knows our intent.

If you have the gift of tongues, you can pray in the Holy Spirit. Tongues represent the direct language of heaven. Your prayers are sent up to God attached to spiritual wisdom of those things past, present, and future. The Holy Spirit is watching for you. If you do not have the gift of tongues, put your whole being into your prayers—mind, body, and spirit—including watching and praying that you never leave God's path. According to Matthew 36:41, we should "Watch as well as pray so that we do not fall into temptation. The spirit is willing, but the flesh is weak." We must watch so that our flesh and emotions do not take us down the wrong path. We discussed controlling our emotions in chapter 3.

I have found this to be true in my personal prayer life. Watching helps me to ask better for the things I need and desire. Watching and praying helps me to ask God what is His purpose for me. For example, let's say you have two types of single-parent fathers: one is busy running around chasing women and the other is busy trying to be the best single father in the world. Both may believe in God, but the father who is focused on his child is paying attention to every good deed his son does, as well as every mistake. He has noticed that his son's grades have slowly declined since divorcing his mother. It is not a big drop—just that the 90 percent is now 85 percent.

However, because this father is watching, he can foresee what could potentially get worse. This gives him an advantage in his prayer life as he watches and prays. He can block in the spirit what would have the power to manifest in the flesh. Also, he can address the situation with his son; using both prayer and work results in action. If he were too preoccupied like the other father, who is busy chasing skirts, things would be much different because he would not recognize that an issue exists. Nor would he have developed the quietness in his life that is needed for the discernment to pray for small problems before they become big problems. The father who pays attention can hear his son's silent cries.

Perhaps you are in a relationship with someone who appears to be nice, but because you have been hurt in relationships several times before, you guard your heart. You notice that they are not calling you as much this month. Instead of flying off the handle and cursing them out, you take it to God in prayer. You ask Him to reveal what the issue is and to give you the correct words to confront the issue. After you have prayed, the Lord leads you to make a nice candlelit dinner for you and your significant other. The two of you do not live together, so you invite them over. After dinner, you take them by the hands, look them in the eyes, and tell them how much you love them while expressing your concern. They get choked up and tell you that their mom is in the hospital. They begin to explain why they have been distant and didn't want to put their burden on you.

Now, imagine if you had not waited patiently and had become offended and rude, thinking it was all about you (which a lot of us do). Your reaction could have made things a lot worse. The definition of watch according to the Oxford Dictionary, is to "look at or observe attentively, typically over a period of time." A period of time means to watch and not make quick judgments that might lead you astray.

1 Peter 5:8 tells us, "Be sober, be vigilant; because your adversary the devil, as a roaring lion, walks about, seeking whom he may devour." Watching helps us to protect ourselves from danger and harm. Watching allows us to discern situations, discern people, and discern ourselves. Watching helps us to make better decisions instead of just going on impulses when choosing a mate, school, or career. It is in our best interest to watch how our lives are playing out in those areas and how people are treating us, how we are treating ourselves, how people are responding to us, and the best way to respond to them. This will lead us into all truth, because when we watch we gain wisdom. John 15:7 says, "If ye abide in me, and my words abide in you, ye shall ask what ye will, and it shall be done unto you."

Watch Yourself

Although it is important to pay attention to others, I believe it is critical that we watch ourselves. When we were growing up, we always had someone watching over us. As young children we were never left unattended (I hope). When I was a young girl, my grandmother would get dressed up just to sit on the sun porch in her wooden rocking chair and watch me ride my pink bike with the white banana seat. Grandma would watch me ride up and down the block. However, since we've become adults, most of us no longer have that parent or guardian who will keep us safe from danger and harm.

Before my grandmother passed away, she told me when I was around fifteen that "No one can take care of Shawntá like Shawntá can take care of Shawntá." Grandma was telling me that you have to look out for yourself, watch out for yourself, provide for yourself, and nurture yourself. Grandma stressed that no one could do a better job of that than me. She wanted me to understand that I was the one in charge of making sure I was well taken care of.

Although my grandmother did not finish the third grade, she had the wisdom of centuries. I recall old and young women and men from the neighborhood coming to visit her looking for answers and suggestions for their lives. Her opinion was respected and *expected*, whether things were going wrong or right in the lives of others. She planted seeds in me as a child that I continue to water every day. I never forgot her words. No matter what circumstance I was in or how low I got, when I was not wise enough to watch or pray, I was able to remember what Grandma said. Because of those very words, I could not look to doctors to save me when I was going through my mental storm. I could not look to my mom to help me through my depression. I could not look to a friend to help me get through school after I had gotten expelled.

I had to look at myself and say, "I am going to be the one who gets me out of this situation. It is going to be me making a decision, and it is going to be God moving on behalf of my faith." That thought process—watching myself, making the decision to overcome, and praying—has delivered me from so many difficult situations in my life. It will deliver you out of any darkness as well.

If you ever have children, you must watch and take care of yourself first before you are able to take care of that child the way they need to be taken care of. Even before the child is born, a mother is told to take folic acid, eat healthy foods, and abstain from drugs and alcohol so the baby will grow to be healthy and strong.

Watching yourself also involves watching over your thoughts, making sure that you are thinking about the right things. It means evicting doubt and fear from your thoughts, and replacing them with faith, victory, and courage. Watching over yourself includes taking care of your emotions, taking time out for yourself when you are getting stressed. It means removing yourself from unhealthy situations and unhealthy people. It means not allowing anyone to abuse your heart or feelings and take you for granted, knowing you deserve to be treated like the queen or king God made you to be, and not settle for less.

Watching over yourself means making sure that you regularly exercise, eat a balanced diet, and take soothing baths—doing all you can to put yourself at ease and at peace so that you are energized and replenish the energy you may have lost.

Watch the Mate You Choose

Your circle of influence is called that for a reason. The people you surround yourself with have the power to influence you in a positive or negative way. A friend can bring you way down, and the person you choose to love can bury you and your dreams if you choose the wrong person to nurture your heart.

In my late teenage years and even early twenties, I was guilty of allowing myself to be naïve and deceived by men who were extremely attractive or could buy me what I wanted. I was twenty years old when I "officially" dated my first drug dealer. He had a big personality, the life of the party, but most salespersons are like that. I was in my third year of college when he and I met; the fake friend who dated my ex hooked us up. I should have known not to take seriously anyone referred by her, but my loneliness and lack of discernment and prayer life led me in his direction.

He and I rode around from crack house to crack house. We made quick parking lot transactions and even sometimes sat in the crack houses for hours just selling drugs. I can recall going into the house of a guy named Bill, a middle-aged white guy with dark hair, kinda thin. He worked every day and had a really good-paying job. He was also a single father of a five-year-old, adorable blue-eyed girl. The sad part was that Bill was on crack, and he was on it bad. He would give us his car for the day just for one rock to smoke, and he would miss work just for the hit. We sometimes had his car for weeks.

One day when I was sitting in his kitchen chair reading a book to his daughter, he looked at me and said, "You seem like a really nice girl. Don't let these guys out here ruin your life." He gave me a lot to think about after I left. I remember going back to Bill's house and sitting in the car as my boyfriend ran into the house to make a deal, thinking, "Is this my destiny? Is this the future intended for me? Is this my fate?" My mind went back to growing up in the projects with my mom on drugs and addicts running in and out of my house. I thought to myself, "Yeah, it all makes sense. I am supposed to be the girlfriend of a big-time drug dealer and the first lady kingpin of my city; together we can build an empire."

I was clearly out of the will of God for my life, and I could feel it nagging at my spirit. The man I chose to be in a relationship with had led me away from God's plan for my life. I had become what society destined me to be, a product of my environment. I became a bigger extension of my problem and not the solution. I was no longer in the program of drugs and crime in my community, but I was an official board member. Lost and confused, I became unmotivated, depressed, and began drinking heavily and smoking weed.

That relationship led me into the wrong places and around the wrong people, who did not have my best interests at heart. It took me a whole year to get out of that relationship. Much crying and praying, ignoring his phone calls and loud pounds on my door. I knew somewhere, deep down inside of me, that this was not the path for me. I had lost my way. I truly believe that relationship would have ultimately destroyed me had I not given myself to God and gotten saved. You see, no matter how far you are from God, and no matter how many mistakes you make, once you accept Jesus into your heart, He never leaves you. God promises, "I will never leave you nor forsake you" (see Deuteronomy 31:6). He sends His messenger, the Holy Spirit, to witness to us, cling to us, and counsel us as we go about life.

When we choose a mate, we end up loving that person, and when you love someone you tend to *fall in love*. That also means falling into whatever they are into, good or bad. You must choose wisely, watch, pray, and protect your heart. The Bible tells us in Proverbs 4:23 to guard our heart for this very reason.

Give your heart to someone who will celebrate your talents, your uniqueness, your gifts and accomplishments. One who will celebrate with you on the way to each blessing God has for your life. Watch and pray that they will love you right, that they are courteous, kind, and loving, that they will pray for you and pray with you. We all deserve someone who nurtures us, treats us with respect, and elevates our self-esteem.

Watch the Friends You Choose

I admit, when it comes to friends, good ones are hard to find. Of course, you can find someone to hang out with, share a movie and a funny story with, but a real friend is one you can share secrets with, confide in, and trust. A friend is someone who is honest with you whether you are right or wrong. If you are wrong, they do not have a problem letting you know. That is a true friend.

Whenever I speak of friends or see someone with a best friend, I almost always tell those friends to cherish each other and let no one or nothing separate them. I have a strong passion when it comes to the bonding of friends because I lost my best friend to AIDS at a very young age. He was twenty-three.

He and I were best friends since the age of ten. At the start, he had a small crush on me but was in no way my type (I was into the rough guys), so we just called each other brother and sister. It's funny, because our friendship started with him telling on me. You may be wondering how I became friends with a tattletale? Trust me, I wonder the same thing—even to this day. It all started when he and a young boy I had a crush on came to my house. You could say he was my boyfriend. At the end of a Nintendo game, my ten-year-old boyfriend wanted to say goodbye with a kiss, so he and I held hands and went to the side of the house by my living room window. We held each other's hands, closed our eyes, and went in for that adolescent peck on the lips—*mwah!*

Immediately after the kiss, I heard my soon-to-be best friend scream from inside the living room window, "Ohh, I am telling your mom!" *Bam!* I smacked my boyfriend in the face (I still don't know why I hit him) and ran into the house to try and stop him from telling on me. My efforts were unsuccessful, and I was grounded for two weeks—I could not go outside or talk on the phone. My mom only allowed one of my friends, who had won her heart over, and that of course was my best friend.

I disliked the very sight of him and wanted nothing to do with him, slamming doors in his face and stomping all the way down the hallway like I was in a marching band when my mom let him in. I know he probably had his selfish, jealous motives for ratting me out, but from that act he became the big brother I never had. After I had gotten over the pain of betrayal, we were the best of friends. Just a couple years before he died, he confessed to me that he was gay. It did not change my love for him one bit. In fact, I was waiting for him to feel brave enough to tell me. He was still a child of God and my big brother regardless.

I share this story with you because although he knew I would be mad at him for ratting me out, he did the right thing. I should not have been kissing. Period. That is what best friends do, protect you at all cost, even if it means protecting you from yourself. I did the same for him and accepted him for who he was—whether I agreed or not was not important. I was leaving that in God's hands.

So how do we choose our friends? Just because someone wants to be our friend is not a reason to be their friend. I knew my friend had my best interest at heart, so I trusted him. I later shared secrets, and he kept them. He took up for me in school if someone said something about me that he did not agree with, and I did the same thing for him.

However, there are people out there in the world who want the title of our friend but lack the actions and hide the motives of their heart. Beware, because there are those who want to get near you to use you, hurt you, and belittle you. They secretly despise everything about you or have some hidden agenda.

Let's take Judas, for instance. He was one of the twelve disciples chosen by Jesus to help Him carry out the mission of God. Judas was called a friend, and Jesus treated him with love and respect, no different from the other disciples. He hurt Jesus by betraying Him and even giving Jesus a kiss that led to His arrest and crucifixion. This same Judas had stood by Jesus's side, walked with Him, and talked with Him. Judas prayed with Jesus, ate with Him, and watched Him perform many miracles. But when the opportunity came for Judas to make his profit, he sold Jesus out. The incredible thing about the deception of Judas is that it was all part of God's plan. Judas was used by God so that prophecy could be fulfilled. Jesus died so that we might have a life. Jesus overcame Judas and ultimately overcame the world (John 16:33). Maybe someone took advantage of you or manipulated and deceived you. Don't worry; Genesis 50:20 reminds us that what they meant for evil, God turns around for our good.

We need friends and loved ones who are going to help us in this race of life. The Bible says the race is not given to the swift or the strong, but to the one who endures to the end. But how can we ever get to the end if we allow ourselves and others to place stumbling blocks in our paths? We cannot. In the race called life, we all need people running with us side by side, cheering us on, handing us water bottles, and saying encouraging words. We need people who will push us to keep going forward.

So I'll tell you like my grandma told me: no one can take care of you like you can take care of you. So take care and watch over yourself. Pray and allow God to watch over you in heaven as well as on earth. Pray that He surrounds you with people who have your best interests at heart. Remember, you have the power in Christ to overcome the battle within and the people who wish you harm. No weapon formed against you shall prosper.

Let us continue to watch and pray, keeping our hearts pure from all malice and anything that's not from God. Matthew 26:41 tells us, "Keep watch and pray so that you will not give way to temptation." Watch and pray that your heart is pure, repenting and making sure you have an honest relationship with God. Doing so will help you cope with and overcome your personal struggles and live a life of love and peace. Read your Bible and watch your actions, making sure they line up with the Word of God. Stay on the positive path leading to a prosperous, righteous future, on earth and in heaven.

 **Closing Prayer**

Holy Spirit, visit me each day and remind me to pray. As I rise, give me the spirit of thanksgiving and communication with You. Lord, open my eyes so that I may see the truth, and reveal unto me the true intentions of everyone around me. Lead me. Guide me, and protect my loved ones and me. Help me to slow down and take my time as You lay Your wisdom upon me in my decision making and judgment. Jesus, I trust You as my guide. Allow me to see into the spirit realm, and protect my spirit from all people, places, and things that are not of You. I welcome wisdom, knowledge, and understanding into my soul. Today and this day forth, daily prayer and meditation on Your Word will be my way of life. In Jesus's name, I watch and pray. Amen.

Chapter 7

God in the Dark

You are never too far gone. I know this because in my darkest moment, God was there. How could He have come for me after all I had done? Through all of my pride, self-righteousness, and unforgiveness? How could He come to my rescue after I had turned away from Him and no longer found it necessary to acknowledge Him as Lord of my life? I had falsely discovered my life and agenda were too much for me to stop and pray. How could He still love me in spite of all my sins? As I sat alone after being delivered from my personal hell, I heard a small voice say, "Because I love you. You left Me, but I made you a promise that I will never leave you nor forsake you" (see Deuteronomy 31:6).

The day I was awakened by His presence showed me how far I was from Him. It was like trying to connect to your favorite radio station with no antenna. There had been so much static and fizziness in my life—dealing with the wrong people, making unwise decisions, too much drinking, drugs, and bad relationships. I could hear His voice, but the words were not clear. I could feel His presence, but it was so hard to connect with Him.

March 4, 2000…I will never forget the day. It is sort of astonishing how I can remember every little detail despite being so lost and confused. I was twenty-one years old at the time and got invited by a few friends to go to a very popular corner bar in my old neighborhood. Once we got there, we ordered our favorite drinks and found a table to sit at. Looking back, I really had no business being in that type of bar. It was filled with drug dealers and prostitutes and was known for violence. But like I said, it was a popular spot so we wanted to be in the mix of things.

As we were sitting at the table I had to go to the bathroom really bad—I guess from all the water I drank prior, trying to combat a future hangover. So I asked my friend if she could watch my drink. She said yes as she was snapping her fingers and dancing in her chair to the music. When I returned from the bathroom, everyone was on the dance floor and my drink was left there unattended. I couldn't believe my friend had left my drink there like that. My thoughts went back to one of the many life lectures my mom gave me when I was a young girl. I could hear her saying, "Shawntá, when you start going out, never leave your drink; always take it with you, even to the bathroom."

That night I wish I had heeded her wisdom; instead I thought, *Well, the dance floor is not far from the table…I'm sure she looked over her shoulder a few times.* I picked up the amoretto and sour and downed the entire thing. Suddenly, the room started to spin. I got a burst of energy and felt unstoppable, invincible even. I recall seeing one of my best childhood friends upset, and when I asked her what was wrong she told me that the two girls standing by the door—identical twins—were talking about her, and how they had jumped her and beat her up pretty badly a month prior.

Now this girl was one of the toughest chicks in our neighborhood growing up. She was known for fighting and winning. I stood there subconsciously reminded of all the times she had jumped in fights for me when there was more than one girl trying to attack me. In a rage, I ran toward the door fearless, not caring that there were two against one. I blacked out for some time, and when I came to I was standing outside in the front of the bar in the grass. One twin was on the ground and the other was holding her head and standing nearby with an audience of people between us yelling loud and swearing as if they were watching a UFC fight.

The friends I had come with had left me behind, so I flagged down a guy I knew from school for a ride. He told me he knew which club they had gone to next. Still seeing the colors and flashes of lights all around from whatever was in my drink, I told him to drop me off there. I went inside in search of the girl who left my drink. Everyone there came from the previous bar, so they all saw the fight and led me into the bathroom straight to her. I kicked open the door of her stall and dragged her out. My anger was at an all-time high, and whatever was in that drink had driven me mad. The look in my eyes must have been a scary sight because I remember hearing my friend scream, "Look at her! She's going to kill me!" The ladies were yelling, "Get her!" while the men were yelling, "Tay, don't do it!" Although I was out of it, the nature of my heart kicked in and I listened to the men and let her go. She ran out of the club crying.

As for me, I stayed there with the crowd that night hallucinating and tripping as I walked back and forth through the club. Later I found myself on the dance floor dancing with the devil—a pure spirit of evil dancing across from me—and as I've reminisced on that night, I realize that his disposition did not fit the club. The age group of the club was about twenty-one to twenty-five, and the music was strictly modern rap and hip-hop. This man was between fifty and sixty years old with a long beard and piercing eyes. He was smiling at me the entire time with a devilish grin as if he were pleased with the state I was in. It reminded me of the story of Jesus when He was tempted in the wilderness by the devil. However, in my case, this man responded the way the devil might have if Jesus had been weak and taken him up on his offer. That dance that night was evidence that I had made many wrong decisions that led me two-stepping into a mental and spiritual hell. Perhaps I was the only one who saw the devil that night because of the state I was in, but spiritually the dance we shared was an accurate reflection of what I was experiencing in my soul.

After that night, I was up for about four days straight pacing the floor with racing thoughts and feeling a dark cloud all around me. There were people at my house that day, and someone offered me some weed to smoke. I was told it would help to calm me down, but after two puffs I experienced what the doctor called a brief psychotic episode.

Suddenly I felt a heaviness on my spirit, as if I had just been introduced to a spiritual curse that had been placed on my family way before I was born. At that time, I didn't know much about the gift of discernment, but it seemed as if mine shifted into high gear. I looked at my mother and asked her if there was anything peculiar she had been holding onto that was given to her from someone in the family. She ran into her room and brought me some old dimes she had been keeping in her jewelry box. She told me her father, my grandfather, had worn them around his ankles to block curses from entering his body. She then shared with me that he never changed the dimes and this was when he had gotten ill and died.

In a panic I replied, "What else?" I started looking around the house for more superstitious symbols and things that did not reflect Jesus. I prayed out loud and praised God, asking Him to save me and my family from this curse. My skin was becoming hot as I continued to walk up and down the hallway. My mother could see I was fighting a spiritual battle. She ran back to her room and grabbed some holy water from under her bed and splashed it on me as she prayed.

My thoughts raced and suddenly I questioned everything I used to believe in. It was almost as if I was searching for the ultimate answers to life. After about two hundred questions, the final answer I came up with that stopped the flood of thoughts was…love. The questions stop at that final answer. My senses became sharper. I could smell things far away. As I went outside, it seemed like I could smell the flowers a block away and the guy walking up the street two blocks away; I could even smell his cologne. I started to run, putting up both hands to the sky and praising God, something I should never have stopped doing four years earlier. I was looking for God and the answer to love but could not see or feel it. I recall thinking to myself: "Something is not right with me." I could remember Sister Lou and my grandmother talking when I was a little girl coming in for prayer meetings, saying: "When it's the end of the world, all you have to do is look up and call the name Jesus, and no matter where you are or what you are doing, you will be saved."

I looked up to the clear blue sky, and with both arms raised up I cried "Jesus!" But nothing happened. He did not come down immediately and take me out of my mental storm, so I decided to try and find Him on my own. I took off running as fast as I could in search for Jesus. Barefoot, running like the bionic woman, there I was running down the street, dodging cars and glass on the ground. I could not find Him. I was caught in the storm and could not get out. I was trapped.

A friend of my mother's came out to follow me and to make sure I didn't get hurt. He ushered me back to my mom's house and called the ambulance. The running continued when I got to the hospital, but now I realized I had put myself in a spiritual fight. I belonged to God, but I had flirted with the devil, so he too was there to claim his rights for my soul, much like the devil tried to claim the body of Moses. As I slowly calmed down, the nurse asked for my name. I looked at her and knew what my name was but could not say it out of fear they would take my identity, as I had let people take my identity in the past, which I believed led me to the hospital.

I was aware of the damage I had caused myself by sharing myself with the wrong people. I was aware, in that moment, that I had allowed myself to be taken down the wrong road and was paranoid. I knew not to share myself ever again, not even my name. I knew why I was there, but I could not verbalize it. Not telling them my name made my mental state appear even worse, so I was admitted into what I call my purgatory—a place or state of suffering inhabited by the souls of sinners who are expiating their sins before going to heaven.

They placed me in the mental health department of the hospital in a place called "constant care." This was for patients who needed the most service and much attention. Because I was still a woman of faith, my discernment was very high, and I realized that I was in a spiritually lost place, filled with some families who had been cursed, unforgiving souls, murderers, and individuals involved in witchcraft.

One lady would not leave me alone. She was up in my face the moment I got there screaming, "Who are you? What are you doing here?" and even wrote those exact words on a picture of mine that my mother had dropped off during a visit. This older, very big-eyed, dark-skinned black woman would continually look at me and scream, "I do not know you!" One time she tried to attack me, and I had a cup of water that I prayed over in my hands and threw it on her. I was hoping she would melt like the wicked witch from *The Wizard of Oz*. But because I had tried to cool her down with my prayer water, the staff placed me in a small room alone as a form of punishment.

In that room, I exercised and wrote poetry to pass the time. There was a small window on the door just about the size of my face, and the woman who tried to attack me earlier put up a white napkin with what appeared to be blood on it. She looked at me with a warm smile. At that time, she appeared totally different in demeanor. Her face showed peace, and the look in her eyes seemed to reveal that she knew me, the total opposite of what she had shown me before I threw my prayer water on her.

I believed that because I had put the holy water on her with faith, she would leave me alone. God revealed to her who I was, a child of God who had given her life to Christ. God had given her a message to tell me, and that message was to remind me that the blood covered me. I got the message.

God has a way of speaking to you through the people you least expect. He does not discriminate. Never let the appearance, age, gender, race, location, or even mental state, in my case, keep you from receiving a spiritual sign, word, or message that God wants you to have. God uses all things and all kinds of people—sinners and all—to get you to Him. You are never too far gone.

I thank God that when I was a young girl my mother and grandmother included me in prayer and worship services with Sister Lou. I am so glad that I accepted Jesus into my life at the tender age of twelve. I am thankful I was wise enough to attend Bible study and church to learn about God and all His miraculous works and great power. When you give your life to God, it cannot be taken away. It is like having a car wreck and damaging your car, but having insurance for eternity. Although I put myself there because of bad choices, I had insurance. I was covered in the blood of Jesus, and this woman in the mental hospital was right there to remind me of just that.

The revelation she imparted can be found in Exodus 12:13: "The blood will be a sign for you on the houses where you are, and when I see the blood, I will pass over you. No destructive plague will touch you when I strike Egypt." I had been reminded of God's promise.

The hospital let me out of the small room the next day, and I can remember praising God up and down the hallway. Now they already thought I was crazy, so I am sure their notes at the end of the day tried to analyze this behavior. Nonetheless, I continued praising God while I was at my worst. However, I found joy in knowing that God was there, right there with me. After I had finished praising Him, I sat against the wall and reality set in. I became depressed, and my face was wet with tears. I was coming around and knew just where I was and how my actions had led me to this dark place.

As I cried I repented to God, but I also repented to myself. I could feel the chains of darkness begin to break from my spirit, although I was still a little confused about my surroundings. Then suddenly this older lady with very large wrinkled hands and a small hump on her back started running toward me screaming, "Something is going on, something is going on, what is happening to you? Stop it, stop it!" She dove at me, and immediately four guards with white gloves grabbed her, but she put up a mean fight and stared at me with hate in her eyes. They strapped her down and gave her a shot, and she slowly calmed down.

When I look back, I believe she knew I had been delivered from that place that very moment, but something in her did not like it. When we give our lives to God, not everyone will be happy or celebrate our growth as we change and decide to walk with God. We will be attacked because the enemy does not want to see us free. The Bible says the devil is here to steal, kill, and destroy, but I (Jesus) come that you may have life and have it more abundantly.

The devil will do all in his power to set you off track and distract you with problems and negative people because he does not want to see you succeed. He especially doesn't want you to receive the promises of God and fulfill your life's purpose, but let me fill you in on a secret. *He cannot stop it.* No matter how low you get, how much sin you have committed, how many lies you have told, and all the things you want to hide, once you have accepted Jesus into your life, He will deliver you, but you have to call on Him and repent.

The very next day, they let me out into a larger community. I was able to attend groups and run track. I attended sessions to get to the root of some of my childhood pain and poor choices. I was on my way until the manipulator—patients who had created their own religion—came. They wanted to fill me in on it. My spirit knew it was a trap, so I continued reading my Bible and successfully passed all my evaluations and was released back into my life. The first thing I noticed was how beautiful the sky was. I admired all things natural: the lake, grass, flowers…and butterflies followed me for just about the rest of that summer, as if telling me to fly. I had been birthed and indeed I would. I would fly to God and never leave His side. He is a God of second chances, and my life rightfully belonged to Him.

When I called on the name of Jesus at the beginning of my storm, He did not come through immediately, but I now understand that He wanted me to go through the storm for a reason. The Bible says, **"He never puts more on you than you can bear."** I never thought I would get through the storm; each day was a struggle, but Jesus was there all along, encouraging me, motivating me, guiding me, protecting me, leading me, strengthening me, and molding me. He molded me into the founder/CEO, inspirational speaker, life coach, advocate, and author I am today. Most importantly, I am a living witness of God's power.

After the storm had cleared the Holy Spirit revealed to me why my racing thoughts stopped at the beginning of my breakdown with the answer…love. It is because God's greatest commandment is: "'Love the Lord your God with all your heart and with all your soul and with all your mind.' This is the first and greatest commandment. And the second is like it: 'Love your neighbor as yourself'" (Matthew 22:36-40). From that day forward, there is no love greater in my life than my love for God; without Him I can do nothing but with Him I can to all things. What I had to endure was not easy. I would not wish anything like that on anyone, but to know God like I know Him now and to live every day walking in my purpose and in His power, it was all worth it. Because of Christ all things have worked out for my good, and if you place your trust in God and keep Him first, He will do the exact same thing for you.

Let me remind you, wherever you are in life and whatever you are going through: nothing is too hard for God. He is right there with you. In Psalm 139:8 David said, "If I ascend into heaven, thou art there: if I make my bed in hell, behold, thou art there." God not only answers His name in the dark, but He will sit right next to you, hold your hand, lift you up, and carry you through. You are never too far gone.

Closing Prayer

Lord, there is nothing too hard for You. I know You will meet me right here where I am imperfect, a sinner. No matter how hard or how low I fall, You are there to meet me and catch me with open arms. Psalm 139:8 says, "If I ascend into heaven, thou *art* there: if I make my bed in hell, behold, thou *art there*." Lord, hold me in Your arms, wipe my tears, my fears, my pain, and my sins away. I come to You just as I am in confidence knowing You can and will put together my broken pieces. Remove all guilt and shame that is upon me because You are my Father; You only see me as Your loving child. Father, I am calling out to You, and I know You are here right now, answering my prayer. Thank You for being here in my darkest hour, providing me with strength, knowledge, power, and wisdom. I thank You for Your grace, mercy, and everlasting love. Take me out of the dark into Your marvelous light and everything great You have planned for me. In Jesus's name, amen.

Chapter 8

God Will Give You a New Name

Isaiah 56:5 declares, "I will give them within the walls of my house a memorial and a name far greater than sons and daughters could give. For the name I give is an everlasting one. It will never disappear."

After I had been released from the hospital, the journey was long and restless. I was not clear as to where I would go from there. I had no idea how God would ever melt me—a flat damaged piece of clay—and mold me into the woman of God I am today. There's a gospel song that says, "Little becomes much when you place it in the Master's hands." I am living proof of this. I endured many days of fear about what the day or tomorrow would bring, sleepless nights, and anxiety. I did not understand what had happened to me. I had so many questions, but the doctors seemed to be just as confused as I was.

First they said I was bipolar, also called manic depressive. Then they said I was depressed and finally determined I just had a brief psychotic episode. All I knew was that I could not sleep, and I feared it would happen again because no one could explain anything to me. They pretty much just dropped me off into society with no closure. I had only been a commuting college student and knew nothing about shopping, paying bills, and living on my own. The guy I was dating when I got out of the hospital had just been released from jail. We got an apartment together. I was still an intelligent young woman and had a pretty extensive resume even without completing my college degree. So I decided to step out on faith and apply for a job at the health department as an AIDS-HIV social worker.

Even with all my past experiences and personal mistakes, my background consisted of helping others, so that is what I wanted to do. I got hired that very same day. They gave me a large office, and I had my very own work picture badge. I was so happy and proud of myself. After my training it was time for me to practice my presentation in front of my colleagues, and I struggled to do so because my past had stolen my confidence. I was a different Shawntá. The Shawntá in college had no limits, she was fearless, and she broke down color barriers and went after hard things.

But now I was empty. There I was, trying to give a presentation, thinking to myself that I was not worthy. The voices of negative self-talk grew so loud I would stop and sit down right in the middle of my lecture. I remember one of my good colleagues, Steve, saying, "There's no wrong way to do the right thing." Those words were powerful, but at that time I did not hear them because of how I felt about myself. A person can share how they feel about you, give you accolades and praise, but at the end of the day all that matters is how you feel about yourself.

My lack of confidence ignited my fears and led me to quit. Not long after, I broke up with my boyfriend. A best friend of his had gotten out of jail and was leading him down the wrong path. He started selling drugs and coming in the house late at night. I was friends with his best friend's girlfriend, so I would hang out at her place and we would talk about how pathetic the two of them were. We never considered that we were a reflection of them because we allowed ourselves to stay in the relationships.

One night we started drinking and eventually talked ourselves to sleep. About 5 a.m. our boyfriends walked in the door smelling like weed and cheap perfume. I jumped off the couch and asked them where they had been so late. My boyfriend replied, "Out making money." I was pretty much fearless when it came to confrontation and violence because I was at such a low point in my life. I felt I had nothing to lose.

There I stood, 5'2", yelling and screaming at a 6'3", 275-pound Sicilian heavyweight boxer. I yelled, "Where is the money!" I pushed him and pushed him again. As he tried to exit through the door, I followed him. His best friend's girlfriend was passive and shy, but she followed right behind me. Once we got outside, the arguing became louder and louder, then out of nowhere he grabbed me and slammed me to the concrete, right on my back. I was in so much pain; I could barely move.

My friend knew by the look on my face that I was hurt. She ran into the kitchen as I was getting up and secretly gave me a knife. Lord, why did she do that? As soon as she gave it to me, I ran up to him and stabbed him in the right side of his chest. He looked stunned, unable to believe I had stabbed him. I dropped the bloody knife and ran into the house to gather my things and go home. His friend drove him to the hospital, where he was treated for minor injuries. He came back to the apartment the next day with a smile, saying that he loved me. I said that I loved him too, but I knew deep inside that I had to work on me, and I could not accomplish that work if I stayed with a man who brought out the worst in me. I moved out and went back home to stay with my mom.

It was still a little wild at my mom's house at the time. Mom was still drinking, and of course I had a few, sometimes one too many. I can recall one time I went out drinking, and a guy followed me home and tried to enter my bedroom. Thank God my mom was there to intervene and put him out. I was still on medication at the time, so the alcohol did not make matters better.

I wanted my own place, so I decided to apply for public housing and was denied. My uncle told me to appeal my request. At the hearing, I shared my story and was granted housing. I had a few doctors' appointments where I had to fill out paperwork, and on one occasion, after I turned them in, I could hear two ladies talking and laughing. One of them spoke my name and said to her friend, "She doesn't even know how to spell her own name." I had left the accent out at the end of my name, so she assumed I spelled it wrong. I never forgot about her laughing at me because she assumed I did not know how to spell my name. It revealed to me how cruel people are in the world; I was there for help, not hurt. A stranger felt it necessary to belittle me and make me feel even worse. Little did she know, God had great plans for my name.

My apartment was just one bedroom—very small—but it was mine. I kept it clean and tidy, scrubbing and waxing the floors on my hands and knees, dusting every day, wiping down the walls once a month, spraying Pledge on the wooden kitchen cabinets. I told myself I would take care of what little I did have and did the best I could with $500 a month. I worked many different jobs but eventually quit all of them due to depression. I began to seek God's face like never before, on my knees daily asking Him to heal me, deliver me, and give me a purpose and a new name. I forgave my mother, my father, and even myself for what I had put myself through. I was developing a relationship with God.

One evening, after watching sermons by TD Jakes and Juanita Bynum, I broke out into this spontaneous praise right in my apartment. I began to dance, shout the name of Jesus, clap, and thank God for all

He had done. Suddenly I dropped to my knees and for the very first time spoke in tongues. Rocking back and forth on my knees, I started to cry, and the tongues got louder and louder. I could hear the Holy Spirit whisper to me plead the blood of Jesus over your family from generation to generation from the beginning of time. I began pleading the blood over my families health, finances, relationships, peace..etc. wherever I knew a problem existed that I witnessed or heard about, I casted it out that night. God's power was already in my life, but now He would give a new meaning to my name and a new meaning to my life's purpose. There I was, in the presence of God, face-to-face. My final prayer was very simple: "Lord, bless me to be a blessing."

I was thinking just bless me enough to have all my needs met financially and to help my family members in need. However, God had a plan and His plan was to use me, to change my name and make it great on His behalf. You will soon discover, just as I have, that greatness comes from serving others. Matthew 23:11 teaches us that the greatest among you will be your servant.

God answered my prayer. At the time I was working for one of the largest employers in my city. One day the Lord spoke to me and said, "I want you to heal others as I am healing you." I was a little reluctant because I was still not fully healed myself. I ask the Lord *why me?* I was still in the wilderness and had not finished college. I still lacked the confidence I'd had in my past, but God did not care what I thought and sent the Holy Spirit as a counselor and comforter for me. The Holy Spirit gave me all the confidence I needed, but unlike in the past, my confidence was not in Shawntá but in God.

Enlightened by this revelation, I was unstoppable and on a mission. I went to the library and began writing about the needs and the pain I saw and personally experienced as a young woman living in my community. Before I knew it, I had a ten-page case that was later turned into a full business plan. I was in front of crowds giving presentations on the need for my self-esteem program for girls. I was lobbying elected officials and joining groups where my voice could be heard and supported by other leaders. The favor I received was supernatural. A university reached out to me and wanted to provide me with free data and statistics on teenage pregnancy and juvenile delinquency.

At the time, Erie County, where I lived, had the highest teen pregnancy and juvenile probations rate in the State of Pennsylvania. I had never known these facts, but God did. I stumbled upon blessings. I never read the newspaper every day, but one particular day I opened it and found an ad from the Community Foundation helping new nonprofits develop their 501c3. The best business plan would be awarded free attorney assistance to incorporate. But you had to be a member and attend their meetings, which ran from 8 a.m. until around 1 p.m.

Keep in mind that I worked a full-time job, second shift, so this was a struggle. I also was taking medication morning, noon, and night. However, at this point it did not matter; the Lord was working and making things happen. I submitted my business plan, and it scored the highest and was awarded full free assistance. This was more confirmation to my spirit that I was in alignment with God. Let me be clear: during this process I had people tell me I was unqualified, I was a black woman, and my plan would not succeed. A large nonprofit even tried to convince me to sell my program, but I refused to give up.

God wanted me to birth it, so in 2006 Nurturing Hearts, a self-esteem and self-development nonprofit organization for at-risk girls, was incorporated. Its purpose is to help young girls who have been physically, mentally, emotionally, and sexually abused growing up in group homes and foster care units. We provide six-month programs and three-day workshops that are geared toward positive self-esteem, healthy lifestyle choices, leadership skills, etiquette, motivational speaking, financial literacy, job placement, educational field trips, and mentoring. Nurturing Hearts holds annual workshops called Beautiful Girls Beauty which teach that beauty is more than what is on the outside. I have taught programs to thousands of girls between the ages of ten and eighteen who have shown great improvements in their grades, school attendance, and behavior, but most importantly, they develop a sense of purpose.

By me obeying God and stepping out on faith, I was down to just half a pill a day of my medication. God was moving me off of dependence on medication to dependence on Him.

After all my success with the youth, I was still uncomfortable sharing what had happened to me and especially about my nervous breakdown. I was not sure if I was ready, so I searched the Scripture for what it had to say about testimony. Revelation 12:11 says: "they triumph over him by the blood of the Lamb and by the word of their testimony." I meditated on this for quite a while. During this time, I was asked to do some presentations for women at the same hospital where I had received mental health treatment. They wanted me to teach women about self-esteem and how to overcome life's obstacles.

I thought, "My God, You are showing me the other side. You are revealing all You have stored up for me. Because I took this leap of faith and trusted You, my curse has been broken." God was showing me, in this new spiritual journey with Him, that I could have life and have it more abundantly (John 10:10). I could hear Him say, "No more fear, Shawntá. Arise, for I the Lord am with you, and I will use you to build faith in others as I have built and healed you." That same year, I started Shawntá Pulliam Arise LLC, providing inspirational speaking, life coaching, and youth and women's advocacy.

God has given me a new name. One that can't be stolen by anyone. He has changed my identity to reflect His power. I no longer have to fear saying my name worried that someone will harm me. I now have confidence and self-esteem not just in myself but in the God who lives within me. No longer am I Shawntá who was expelled from school or Shawntá in the projects or crazy Shawntá. I am Shawntá who overcame,

Shawntá who is healed and delivered, Shawntá who rose from the darkness to help other women and girls heal all around the world—hence Shawntá Pulliam Arise LLC.

Allow God to heal your emotions. Ask Him to help you forgive those who have harmed you, and forgive yourself. Ask Him to lead you back into His arms after you have veered off the path. Allow the Holy Spirit to guide you to watch as well as pray. Let Him help you discern what you should do and where you should go. God answers His name in the dark. He wants to heal your broken pieces and give you a new name. He is there with you wherever you are right now; He is just waiting for you. Always remember that no matter what, God loves you, whether you are in the dust and cannot see or in the dark and unable to find your way. Just call on His name and follow His path because He wants to take you to your destiny.

> *Go from your country, your people and your father's household to the land I will show you. I will make you into a great nation, and I will bless you; I will make your name great, and you will be a blessing.*
>
> Genesis 12:1-2

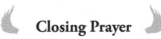

Closing Prayer

God, I now know my life is not my own, but it belongs to You. Let my image be a reflection of You. When people say my name, let it be a name that is attached to Your works and the mission You have placed within me. Allow my mistakes, past sins, and shortcomings to become testimonies that I have overcome and a blessing to those trying to overcome.

Before I had a name and was in my mother's womb, You were with me, planning my blessings and my calling. Give me the power and protection to walk in all that You have stored up for me. Protect me from those who wish to kill, steal, and destroy Your purpose in my life. You said in Your Word that no weapon formed against me shall prosper, and greater is He that is in me than he that is in the world. Today I give my name, my soul, and my spirit—all to you. Rename me. Give meaning and purpose to my name. Let me be a replica of You on the earth. I will do great things for humankind and You, my God. My life is a life of purpose; my name is a name destined for greatness! I break any generational curse that may be upon me and my family, knowing that Your power is far greater than any power against me. I win in You! In the matchless name of Jesus Christ, I plead the Blood amen.

Chapter 9

Life's Good and Bad Leads to Purpose

I t is important that you get saved so you don't stay in the vortex of this world. The Holy Spirit who lives in you once you have given your life to Christ, will rise within you and give you the power and strength to endure whatever may come your way. The Bible says in 2 Corinthians 12:9, "'My grace is sufficient for you, for my power is made perfect in weakness.' Therefore, I will boast all the more gladly about my weaknesses, so that Christ's power may rest on me."

As I look back over my life—all the joy I have experienced, the misfortunes, the lack, the gain, the heartache, the pain, the mistakes, and everything I questioned God about—I have to say that everything

I went through was for a purpose. It was not in vain but rather a part of God's plan, to put me in the place I needed to be.

Psalm 119:71 says, "It is good for me that I have been afflicted: that I might learn thy statutes." This scripture tells us that affliction brings us closer to God when we are lost and trying to find our way. God causes things to happen in our lives to rear us back into His presence, back to the path He designed for our lives. The more I pray and develop a closer relationship with God, the more He reveals to me that it was not just the devil that allowed me to come into the world with an absentee father. It was not a mistake that my mother turned to crack when I was ten. It was not a mistake that I got kicked out of school. It was not the devil alone who put me in the hospital due to a nervous breakdown.

Do not get me wrong; the devil *does* want to kill us and put our lives through hell on earth—as well as in eternity—but he can only do what God allows him to do. If you do not think this is true, just read the book of Job, whom God allowed the devil to afflict to test Job's love and commitment toward God. Satan told God that any man would obey and follow Him if He gave him the desires of his heart and good health, so Job was nothing special. God allowed the devil to put Job to the test by snatching everything he owned from him, but in the end Job stayed faithful to God and passed the test, and Job received more from God than he had before.

When you think you are fooling the people around you, God has a way of showing you that He is real, and in the end He will get the glory for all to see. When I was a young girl, I believed in God but thought some of the prayers were a little funny. All the yelling, raising of hands, and speaking in tongues reminded me of a show. I would smirk as people came over to my grandmother's house to pray. Sometimes their eyes would roll back in their heads. I thought to myself, "What in the world is the matter with her eyes?"

Nonetheless, I was saved at twelve through the influence of Sister Lou, whom I mentioned earlier. She came out to our house, and we prayed and sang hymns as usual, but on this particular day my mom and Sister Lou asked, "Are you ready to get saved?" It was as if they were speaking in slow motion. I was terrified. I had been attending these prayer meetings since I was seven, but I thought I was just a spectator, not a participant. I was not even sure what being saved meant, so I asked. They explained how we are all born into sin and cursed because of the fall of man, beginning with Adam and Eve, and how Jesus came and died only to rise again, delivering us from the curse and giving us everlasting life. He is our Savior and died for all of our sins. I must admit that story was kind of scary to me at the age of twelve, but I was smart enough to realize I'd be worse off if I didn't get saved. So I said, "Yes, I want to be saved!"

Sister Lou had me kneel on the floor in front of her. As she sat there, I put my head down in a praying position, and she placed her hand on top of my head and prayed for my soul. A peculiar fragrance always resonated from Sister Lou. It was not an unpleasant smell but pure and holy. It was a strong fragrance, the signature of her very presence—a smell that reminded you of full protection and surrounding peace. I felt as if I were in the presence of God.

She asked if I would accept the Lord Jesus Christ into my life, my heart, my mind, and if I believed that Jesus died on the cross and rose again. I said yes. She put her hand on my head again and started shaking it with her hand and yelling "Jesus!" while praying. Then she told me to stand up and thank Jesus for what He had done. I knew that I was saved. I could feel it. I felt warm, as though God were very close to me, but it was not the reaction she expected me to have.

Sister Lou told me to jump up and down and say thank you. This was when the performance began. I started jumping up and down as high as I could, like I was on an imaginary trampoline. In my mind, I knew I was faking, so I just took it all the way and mimicked what I had seen others do in the past. I continued to jump up and down. Oh yeah, I had it down to a T and felt like I gave them the show they were seeking.

Later on that night, after she left, I did not feel right about what I had done. I could feel the presence of God and sensed that He was not pleased. I believe that experience marked the beginning of God having to prove Himself a little more to me, to get my attention. This caused me much pain as He delivered and saved me from situations for my faith to grow. He knew just what it would take for me to experience His love, healing, saving, and deliverance, and to break any unbelief that was starting to take root.

Today I am so sensitive to God's presence that I begin to cry thinking of His goodness and where He has brought me from. At times, when I am in deep prayer, Sister Lou's fragrance visits my home, reminding me of His holiness, peace, protection, and presence in my life. He has made me a believer, but I was stubborn, so it took a little more breaking so that He could reveal to me just how strong and powerful He is. Could you be making your life a little harder than it is supposed to be?

I say a little harder because none of our lives will be perfect. Psalm 34:19 even tells us: "Many are the afflictions of the righteous, but God delivers them out of them all." None of us is righteous until we allow God to become first in our lives. I am a living witness that if you put God first, He will deliver you out of the darkness and out of the spirit of defeat that feeds you doubt, worry, and fear. Although struggles may come, you will rest easy knowing that God will not let these situations destroy you. They will make you strong.

I believe that is the difference between someone who is afflicted by God and one who is without God. The one without God treads on to destruction and death, but the one who is with God receives a lesson learned, wisdom, increased strength, and blessings for passing the test. The things I have survived were only a test of my faith so that God could press out the greatness He had stored deep down inside me. I know that many people—family, friends, and strangers—thought it was over for me, with my upbringing, being kicked out of school, losing my best friend, having a nervous breakdown, moving into the projects, and living on disability. I cannot blame them.

I can honestly say that as I was going through all of it, I could not see my way out. However, I came to a point where it did not matter if I could see my way out or not. I began walking blind, taking steps and feeling my way through the darkness, through the clouds of depression and the storm. As long as I was moving forward and continued walking with God, I was going to be all right. I did it afraid, discouraged, confused, lonely, and sad. But I kept going. I did not stop because I could no longer see the light that the poor decisions of my past had obscured; it did not matter. I knew in my spirit that God still lived in me, even in the dark places, the places I was ashamed of. He lived there. I began to see Him turn things around in my life.

Certain things that took place in my life looked bad but because of my rededication, faith, and trusting in Him, I received blessings for the pain, and joy for my tears. When I failed out of school after three years of trying to obtain my college degree due to my illness, He blessed me with a job that only required an associate's degree or similar credits for the position. The first six months of working there, I was still in my healing process. I recall sitting in the breakroom, calming my racing thoughts and battling my anxiety with prayer and deep breathing; tears flooded my eyes as I recited over and over, "Lord, help me. Lord, give me peace," but He heard my cry, answered my prayer, and got me through each day until I was fully healed.

He put an anointing upon me in front of everyone that allowed me to create a nonprofit organization for at-risk girls, just as I once was myself. As I resided in that illusion of despair, I was invited to serve on prominent boards in my community. I developed a partnership with the school district that once expelled me as a child. Then the hospital I was admitted to during the breakdown hired me as a facilitator to speak into the lives of women and help them to heal, believe in themselves, and go after their dreams. From this small beginning, Shawntá Pulliam Arise LLC was birthed.

I believe the position at the hospital awakened my spiritual sense to the mind of God and filled me with a confirmed love and purpose for my life. I stood looking out the large window of the hospital at the beautiful crystal blue waters of Lake Erie. Peacefully, yet suddenly, I realized that was the same window I had looked out during my hospital stay, and at that moment it dawned on me, heavier than before, that God had delivered me, and this journey in life was never about me, but about Him all along. It was about believing in His Word, obeying Him, learning from my mistakes, picking up the pieces, and laying what I had left on the altar.

Today I thank God for being lost, because when I was lost spiritually, it was the start of a new beginning, purpose, and destiny. I now understood the company of the butterflies. He directed them around me at countless times during my brokenness to minister to me of my new birth. I could feel it and accepted the journey.

The journey with God will include joy, tears, accomplishments, mistakes, struggle, victory, failure, and success. However, you will have a constant covering and protection all around you and through you. As you move through this earthly experience, you do not have to do it alone. In fact, it is not meant to be traveled alone; your spiritual Father has not and will not abandon you. Stay with God. He has another side of your pain. He wants to reveal a new path to you—a path that will lead to greatness, prosperity, love, faith, health, peace, strength, wisdom, and joy. There is a purpose for the pain of past mistakes and wrong decisions; everything about you makes up your destiny. Just stay on the path of light. You are filled with God's strength and purpose.

Closing Prayer

God, although I do not fully understand all that I have been through, I choose to believe Your Word that "all things work together for the good to them that love the Lord and are called according to His purpose" Romans 8:28. Lord, you did not say that only the good things work out for my good, but that *all* things, even the bad, the pain, the tears, and the heartbreak. I believe that everything I have lost will be replaced by something better for me. I know and trust that what the enemy meant for evil, it will all work together for my good. Nothing that I have been through will be in vain. You will turn my pain into power. I believe You will use the things I have overcome to be a light and a testimony to help others who are struggling with the same thing. I openly and willingly accept the path that leads to You. As I walk this path, Lord, shield me, protect me, cover me, provide for me, and give me the wisdom and discernment to make the best decisions for my life. I trust what You are working out in my life because I am in Your hands, and Your hands are peace, protection, joy, and love. I remain a winner in You. In Jesus's name, amen.

Chapter 10

Prayer: Fuel for Our Destiny

(Chapter Prayers at a Glance)

The Bible teaches us one very important principle: "In all thy getting get understanding" (Proverbs 4:7). This chapter is a compilation of prayers you can reference after reading each chapter. The purpose is to help you overcome your struggles and embed within your spirit the wisdom and knowledge gifted to you through this book. Saying these prayers will allow God to enter into those areas where you seek a better understanding, healing, breakthrough, and closer walk with Him. I pray that you spiritually master every area you are wrestling with in your life and that God prepares you for the great destiny He has set just for you.

Prayers

Chapter 1 Created for God's Purpose Prayer

Lord, help me to be continually aware of Your presence and unfailing love for me. Whatever I lack in my life, I ask that You fill every void as I lean on and trust in You. Holy Spirit, the Spirit of all wisdom, help me to see, understand, and move on behalf of God's purpose for my life. God does not make mistakes, so I will never be a mistake. I am exactly who God wants me to be. All that I have been through and all that I am will work together for my good and God's perfect plan for my life. I will no longer look at my faults as hindrances, but as steps to where God is calling me to be. I am created for a purpose; my pain will become my power. I believe, I welcome, and I receive the manifestation of God's purpose and destiny for my life. In Jesus's name, amen.

Chapter 2 Veering Away from God Prayer

Lord, help me to draw close to You. I have veered away and know that I am not where You want me to be. Help me not to reject Your love because of the sins and actions of others; help me to remember that You, and You alone, are perfect. There is nothing I can do to separate Your love from me because Your love is eternal and unconditional. Restore my faith in You. Restore my hope in You. Restore my love in You. I invite You back into my heart, mind, and spirit without hesitation or delay. You said in Your Word that You are married to the backslider, and You said in Your Word that You will never leave or forsake me. Lord, forgive me for falling away and abandoning You. I repent. As I wake each morning, I will give thanks for who You are. You are my King of Kings and Lord of Lords; You are my everything. Thank You for being a Father, a friend, and a helpmate in my time of need. From this day forward, I pray that the Holy Spirit will constantly remind me of Your presence, love, and tender care so that I may forever live in Your presence. In Jesus's name, amen.

Chapter 3 Beward of Your Negative Emotions Prayer

O Lord, help me to overcome my emotions and rest in Your presence of peace. Whatever I am feeling, allow me to trust You more than this emotion, knowing there is nothing that I cannot get through when I cast my cares upon You. Help me to rest in You, believe in You, and put all my trust in You. I will not be quick to anger. I will not be quick to fear. I will not allow jealousy or sadness to overtake me. I will acknowledge my emotion but then immediately give it to You. I trust that all things are working out in my favor, and I know that nothing happens that You have not allowed. You said in Your Word that all things work together for the good to them that love the Lord and are called according to His purpose. Lord, no matter what is going on in my life right now, I know that I am called according to Your purpose, and You have peace, love, and joy on the other side of my struggle. As I pray and wait patiently, I receive and thank You in advance for everything good coming my way. In Jesus's name, amen.

Chapter 4 The Art of Forgiveness and the Power Within Prayer

O Lord, give me the strength to let go of this pain deep down inside of me. I want to be free from the torment of [FILL IN NAME] within my thoughts. I refuse to give them power over me because of what they have done. From this day forward, I have no chains binding me. I forgive [NAME] in the name of Jesus. I will no longer be a prisoner of hate and revenge; instead, I ask You to replace them with an inner love and peace within my soul. Lay on me a forgiving spirit. Help me to identify the homelessness in [NAME] and pray for their weakness and illness. As I go through this process, I believe every day I will be healing myself, growing in my spirit, and opening a window of blessings that has been jammed for a very long time because of my unforgiveness. Lord, I pray that every blessing I blocked because of my pain and hatred will be released unto me in the name of Jesus. Fill any void that has been caused by my pain; flood me with Your strength and love. I forgive because You forgave me for my sins, and I want to continue to walk in Your blessings and love. I am free. In Jesus's name, amen.

Chapter 5 Sowing and Reaping

Father, forgive me for any harm I may have caused others or myself. Show me how to take the best care of my body, mind, and spirit. I know my body is Your temple, so help me keep it pure and holy for Your dwelling. Remove any selfish, disrespectful, or inconsiderate ways I may have; pull them out by their roots. Give me a clean heart, one that radiates love through and through. If I have wronged someone, give me a humble spirit so that I may apologize and make it right between that person and me, but most importantly, make my relationship right with You. Instill within me the fruits of the Spirit: love, joy, peace, patience, kindness, goodness, faithfulness, gentleness, and self-control. Let me be a light of joy to others and for myself. Let my actions, words, thoughts, and deeds reflect You. In Jesus's name, amen.

Chapter 6 Watch and Pray Prayer

Holy Spirit, visit me each day and remind me to pray. As I rise, give me the spirit of thanksgiving and communication with You. Lord, open my eyes so that I may see the truth, and reveal unto me the true intentions of everyone around me. Lead me. Guide me, and protect my loved ones and me. Help me to slow down and take my time as You lay Your wisdom upon me in my decision making and judgment. Jesus, I trust You as my guide. Allow me to see into the spirit realm, and protect my spirit from all people, places, and things that are not of You. I welcome wisdom, knowledge, and understanding into my soul. Today and this day forth, daily prayer and meditation on Your Word will be my way of life. In Jesus's name, I watch and pray. Amen.

Chapter 7: God in the Dark Prayer

Lord, there is nothing too hard for You. I know You will meet me right here where I am imperfect, a sinner. No matter how hard or how low I fall, You are there to meet me and catch me with open arms. Psalm 139:8 says, "If I ascend into heaven, thou *art* there: if I make my bed in hell, behold, thou *art there*." Lord, hold me in Your arms, wipe my tears, my fears, my pain, and my sins away. I come to You just as I am in confidence knowing You can and will put together my broken pieces. Remove all guilt and shame that is upon me because You are my Father; You only see me as Your loving child. Father, I am calling out to You, and I know You are here right now, answering my prayer. Thank You for being here in my darkest hour, providing me with strength, knowledge, power, and wisdom. I thank You for Your grace, mercy, and everlasting love. Take me out of the dark into Your marvelous light and everything great You have planned for me. In Jesus's name, amen.

Chapter 8 God Will Give You a New Name Prayer

God, I now know my life is not my own, but it belongs to You. Let my image be a reflection of You. When people say my name, let it be a name that is attached to Your works and the mission You have placed within me. Allow my mistakes, past sins, and shortcomings to become testimonies that I have overcome and a blessing to those trying to overcome. Before I had a name and was in my mother's womb, You were with me, planning my blessings and my calling. Give me the power and protection to walk in all that You have stored up for me. Protect me from those who wish to kill, steal, and destroy Your purpose in my life. You said in Your Word that no weapon formed against me shall prosper, and greater is He that is in me than he that is in the world. Today I give my name, my soul, and my spirit—all to you. Rename me. Give meaning and purpose to my name. Let me be a replica of You on the earth. I will do great things for humankind and You, my God. My life is a life of purpose; my name is a name destined for greatness! In the matchless name of Jesus Christ, amen.

Chapter 9 Life's Good and Bad Leads to Purpose Prayer

God, although I do not fully understand all that I have been through, I choose to believe Your Word that "all things work together for the good to them that love the Lord and are called according to His purpose" (Romans 8:28). Lord, you did not say that only the good things work out for my good, but that *all* things, even the bad, the pain, the tears, and the heartbreak. I believe that everything I have lost will be replaced by something better for me. I know and trust that what the enemy meant for evil, it will all work together for my good. Nothing that I have been through will be in vain. You will turn my pain into power. I believe You will use the things I have overcome to be a light and a testimony to help others who are struggling with the same thing. I openly and willingly accept the path that leads to You. As I walk this path, Lord, shield me, protect me, cover me, provide for me, and give me the wisdom and discernment to make the best decisions for my life. I trust what You are working out in my life because I am in Your hands, and Your hands are peace, protection, joy, and love. I remain a winner in You. In Jesus's name, amen.

About the Author

Shawntá Pulliam took a traumatic childhood, affected by parental drug addiction and incarceration, and turned it around for good. After expulsion from the tenth grade, she was enrolled in Catholic alternative education where she worked diligently to graduate on time. She emerged as valedictorian of her senior class and attended Gannon University. However, Shawntá's unhealed wounds resulted in risky behavior, bad relationship choices, and ultimately a nervous breakdown. She wound up living on $500 a month from Social Security in a one-bedroom apartment in the projects.

Shawntá began to confront her past, acknowledge her wrongs, forgive those who had hurt her, and built a real relationship with God, reclaiming her soul. She started a promising career with G.E. Transportation but still had an unfulfilled passion to help at-risk girls, as she once was.

In 2006, her vision came to fruition when she founded Nurturing Hearts, a self-esteem and self-development nonprofit organization for girls whose mission is to provide supportive leadership and life skills that will furnish and prepare girls ages ten to eighteen for a bright and positive future.

Shawntá Pulliam has not only evolved into a visionary, entrepreneur, motivational speaker, and life coach, she is also secretary of the Erie Policy and Planning Council, a member of the board of directors for the Erie Downtown Partnership, the Truancy Committee, General Electric's African American Engagement Committee, and *Erie Times* News Diversity Committee. She also serves on the Board of Corporators for UPMC Hamot and is a member of the Women's Athena International Power Link.

She is a recipient of the General Electric Gerald L. Philippe Award, the 2013 Women Making History Award, where she received a Citation of Recognition from the Erie County Executive, the 2013 Phoenix Idea Women of the Year Award, the Martin Luther King Youth Impact Award, and she has also been recognized by the governor of Pennsylvania for her outstanding community leadership.

Shawntá recently founded Shawntá Pulliam Arise LLC, through which she provides inspirational speaking, life coach assistance, and positive development programs for people from all facets of life. She has also worked as a facilitator for UPMC, a $10 billion integrated global health enterprise headquartered in Pittsburgh, where she provided inspirational and educational seminars and workshops for women. Shawntá has spoken at small group homes such as the former Gannondale residential facility for girls, and world recognized corporations such as General Electric and the *New York Times* for the DANDI Awards in New York City.

She has been coached by one of the best motivational speakers of all times, Mr. Les Brown, who wrote the foreword to this book.

Shawntá not only "walks the walk" but grabs other young women by the coattails and supports them along the path to success. She has never forgotten children and women who are struggling with the same issues she had to overcome herself. Her message to young women is "the only limitations you have are the ones you place upon yourself," spreading her testimony and enlightenment around the world.

Shawntá lives her life according to Philippians 4:13: "I can do all things through Christ, who strengthens me."

Arise Into Your Destiny

Join Shawnta' Pulliam for

Online and In-Person
Classes, Workshops, and Seminars
Life Coach Sessions
or
Book Shawnta' Pulliam for your next event

For More Information Visit Us At:
www.ShawntaPulliamArise.com

Founded by Shawnta' Pulliam in 2006, Nurturing Heart's, Inc., is a self-esteem and self-development non-profit organization for at-risk girls.

The mission of Nurturing Heart's,Inc., is to provide supportive leadership and life skills, that will furnish and prepare at-risk girls between the ages of 10-18 for a bright and positive future.

We provide 2 day workshops and 6 month programs that focus on:
- Positive Self- Esteem
- Healthy Lifestyle Choice
- Leadership Skills
- Goal Setting
- Financial Literacy
- Motivation and fun career focused field trips!!

For more information about hosting a Nurturing Heart's workshop or program in your city, or to make a contribution towards our mission please contact:

Shawnta' Pulliam 814-460-5954 or
visit www.Nurturing-Hearts.org or
email us at: NurturingHearts05@gmail.com

Contributions to Nurturing Hearts can be sent to:
P.O.Box 653
Erie, Pa 16512

A free eBook edition is available with the purchase of this book.

To claim your free eBook edition:

1. Download the Shelfie app.
2. Write your name in upper case in the box.
3. Use the Shelfie app to submit a photo.
4. Download your eBook to any device.

Shelfie

A **free** eBook edition is available
with the purchase of this print book.

CLEARLY PRINT YOUR NAME ABOVE IN UPPER CASE

Instructions to claim your free eBook edition:
1. Download the Shelfie app for Android or iOS
2. Write your name in **UPPER CASE** above
3. Use the Shelfie app to submit a photo
4. Download your eBook to any device

Print & Digital Together Forever.

Snap a photo

Free eBook

Read anywhere